Training
the Young Actor

Also by MICHAEL R. MALKIN:

Traditional and Folk Puppets of the World

Training
the Young Actor

Michael R. Malkin

Photographs by Wayne Nicholls
Illustrations by Jim Shubin

San Diego • New York
A. S. Barnes & Company, Inc.
In London:
The Tantivy Press

792
MA

Second Edition
Manufactured in the United States of America

For information write to:
A.S. Barnes & Company, Inc.
P.O. Box 3051
La Jolla, California 92038

The Tantivy Press
Magdalen House
136-148 Tooley Street
London, SE1 2TT, England

Library of Congress Cataloging in Publication Data

Malkin, Michael R., 1943-
    Training the young actor.

    Includes index.
    1. Acting—Study and teaching. 2. Children
as actors. 3. Children's plays—Presentation,
etc. I. Title.
PN3157.M34   792'.028   76-50201
ISBN 0-498-01957-8

PRINTED IN THE UNITED STATES OF AMERICA

For my parents, Doris and George

Contents

Acknowledgments

Special thanks are due to several people for their help in preparing this book. I am grateful to Tom Barker of the International Thespian Society, and S. Ezra Goldstein of *Dramatics* for their editorial guidance on material that originally appeared in *Dramatics*, including: "Technicalities: Developing Concentration," November 1976; "Some Simple Tricks for a New Hand," May 1975; "Hands: For More than Applauding," November 1975; "Characterization: Finding and Mixing Primary Rehearsal Units," October 1974; "Facing a Character," May 1974; and "Using Hand Puppets to Develop Skills in Improvisation," November 1973. Additional thanks are due to Jeanette K. Moss, senior editor of *Teacher*, for advice on reworking earlier versions of some chapters, for inclusion in that magazine; to David L. Young for permission to use one of his photographs; to Jim Shubin for his fine illustrations; and to Wayne Nicholls, who took such time and care preparing the photographs for this book.

My greatest debt of gratitude is owed to my wife and colleague, Pam, whose years of professional experience in the field of children's theater have proved invaluable. The lesson plan in Chapter Two is hers. In fact, the entire book was written in close cooperation and collaboration with her. For her intelligence and patience, I offer my gratitude and respect.

Training
the Young Actor

1

More Theater, Less Creativity Please!

Less creativity? That may seem bizarre. But as a teacher of children's theater, I often come into contact with teachers who want or claim to use theater and theatrical games as vehicles for teaching "creativity." Others, who are more adjectival about their purposes, see theater as a way to "help foster creative self-expression" or to help students "develop a creative understanding of themselves and their world." Somewhere along the line, such people usually assume three things. First, theatrical activity is intrinsically creative. Second, theater training and theater games are particularly conducive to the development of creativity. Third, the exercise of a student's creative faculties is the single most important thing that can be achieved through the use of theater in the classroom.

Despite the fact that it may raise a few hackles, I seriously question all three assumptions. In the first instance, theatrical activity is *not* intrinsically creative. Like most arts, theater is a combination of many distinct skills and crafts. These skills can be used artistically—or creatively—but often, even under the best of circumstances, they are not. Any instruction in theater that is not firmly based on the skills and crafts of the art is a contradiction in terms.

In the second place, theater, role-playing games and various kinds of dramatic exercises are no more—or less—conducive to creativity than the ostensibly judicious application of birch rod to backside was to the development of self-discipline in the students of a century ago. Finally, the word creativity itself, through overuse, may have become too weak and vague a term to serve as any kind of educational Holy Grail.

Today's casual overuse of the terms creative and creativity is similar to the unthinking reliance on the word discipline that was so common in an age now fortunately gone by. With relentless frequency, rigid, outmoded and/or insensitive teaching methods were excused, defended, and even extolled on the grounds that they represented disciplined approaches to the processes of teaching and learning. Discipline served as an armor-plated halo that effectively protected those who stood beneath it from often justified criticism. Of course, contemporary teachers tend to be more cautious about the use of the word discipline, and as a partial result are much more alert to the problems and processes of discipline in the classroom.

Just as discipline was once a label that served to conceal or excuse a lot of slipshod thinking and questionable practices, so creativity has become a label or mask for ideas and practices that frequently merit closer scrutiny and further refinement. The subject of this book—the teaching of the skills and crafts of acting to students from seven to fourteen years old—is a topic that is far too often diluted or ignored in the name of creativity.

To my way of thinking, well structured acting programs would be of inestimable benefit in many schools and recreation programs if they were put into the hands of teachers who were knowledgeable and enthusiastic about both the art of acting and the art of teaching acting to children. Just as students between the ages of seven and fourteen can learn to play musical instruments or draw, so can they be taught to act.

The goal of such training need not necessarily be acting for acting's sake. The lessons learned in a properly organized acting curriculum are eminently applicable to a variety of human endeavors and life situations. This book explains a number of techniques for helping to reshape a child's dramatic instincts into acting skills; skills that can be further refined in life as well as art. Acting lessons can be, but seldom are, used to excite certain students about a wide variety of learning experiences including reading and writing skills, the understanding and appreciation of language and literature, training and practice in memory skills, the development of self-confidence and poise and development of the ability to cooperate with others in order to work towards a shared goal.

Nonetheless, instead of improvising a play by performing, writing, polishing, and repolishing an idea in order to develop a suitable script, students are often encouraged to indulge in relatively formless and aimless role-playing (usually called creative role-playing or improvisation). As surprising as it may seem, many teachers make little or no effort to relate the processes of theatrical play-making to the development of their students' reading and writing skills. Hardly ever do they teach anything about stage movement (blocking), characterization or play structure. The ability to memorize—an important skill that develops with use—is frequently discouraged on the sometimes invalid grounds that the learning of lines is too time consuming or authoritarian and tends to stifle creativity, spontaneity, and the free flow of ideas. The likelihood of increasing any student's poise and self-confidence is greatly diffused when public or semi-public performance (performance in front of friends, relatives, and classmates) is discouraged. This is often done amid a welter of questionable assumptions about protection from failure and the sociological strains imposed by performance. Even instruction in basic speech and oral reading skills is circumvented by teachers who assume that theater activity should stress self-expression rather than communication with others.

There is a common misapprehension that acting has more to do with some sort of generalized instinct than with a set of learnable abilities and skills. In other words, the actor is often incorrectly thought of as a *type* of person—brash, outgoing, loud, etc.—rather than as a trained craftsperson. With this thought in mind, teachers can easily rest content teaching nothing about acting because, in their view, there is nothing to teach. Instead, and often with great fervor, they attempt to emphasize the special *creative* flair that they believe is the essence of the art.

Certainly, no one book can hope to reconcile all of the deep-seated disagreements about the nature and purposes of teaching acting to young people. In fact, there are so many divergent beliefs concerning the hows and whys of teaching acting in the classroom that many teachers are justifiably confused. Even among experts, there is little agreement on the definitions of such basic terms as *acting, role-playing, theater* and *creative drama*. Although two people may share the same basic philosophy, they will often disagree when it comes to specific teaching methods. For instance, those who agree that the function of a children's theater curriculum is to teach children about the various arts of the theater, often disagree about the definition of improvisation or the ways in which children should be introduced to such things as characterization or the techniques of stage movement and speech. Others, who see theater in the classroom as a means for stimulating involvement in and enthusiasm for other areas of the curriculum, frequently disagree over whether or not anything at all should be taught about the arts of theater.

The purpose of this book is to explain a number of specific techniques for teaching students between the ages of seven and fourteen about the art of acting. Even those chapters that deal with puppetry, directing, and readers theater are presented as alternate ways of guiding teachers and their students toward a further understanding of the actor's art.

Wherever possible, I have tried to avoid some of the more common problems that teachers have in this area. The first such problem is a continuing reliance on introductory exercises that are most suitable for preschool and primary grade children. Frequently, the same basic role-playing lessons are reintroduced into a child's curriculum year after year by different teachers in scarcely altered form. As a result, an acting or theater curriculum intended for fourteen-year-olds will not be very different from the one offered to the same students when they were seven or eight. By contrast, music teachers—who, unlike theater teachers, are usually highly trained in both education and their art—tend to take a more structured approach. There comes a time, and it usually occurs quite early, when the singing of simple songs, the exposure to different types of music, and the use of elementary musical games, are gradually supplanted by the teaching of how to play specific instruments and how to read music. Unfortunately, in children's theater elementary role-playing games are often continued straight through high school, theater appreciation is rarely taught at all, and students are rarely properly introduced to the basic skills and techniques that good actors should master.

A second, related problem is the widely held conviction that most or many children possess dramatic *instincts* that will develop naturally in the normal course of events. Those who hold this opinion tend to mistake two important elements of the art of acting—the ability to role-play and the ability to imagine vividly—for the total art. As a result, the sum total of a sixth-grade student's experience in theater is likely to be a series of loosely organized imagination and role-playing exercises which have not focused on the introduction to and practice of specific, identifiable acting skills and techniques. At best, the students will have performed a few plays in which the major goal of rehearsals was to get the students to memorize their lines and move about the stage with some semblance of order and cleverness. Under such circumstances, students cannot be expected to learn much about acting.

The acting lessons in this book help students deal with specific acting skills, techniques and problems: analyzing a script, developing a character, moving effectively on stage, speaking clearly and precisely, projecting thoughts and feelings to an audience, and so on.

After students have learned that acting is, in large part, a set of identifiable skills, it becomes somewhat easier to solve one of the most insidious problems faced by children's drama instructors. To put it simply, children are often and honestly cute. As a result, their theatrical failures are frequently more appealing than their successes. Because a student's stage fright, physical uncertainty, or inaudibility can be quite beguiling, particularly to adult audiences, it becomes far too easy for a child to receive positive reinforcement for negative behavior. For example, at a school or camp show an audience is much more likely to applaud or laugh at an obvious mistake (e.g., walking out the wrong exit) or a lapse in memory (e.g., forgetting or jumbling an important speech) than it is to applaud a competent but not quite perfect job. Of course, there is no need to embarrass or punish students for their errors, but there is even less justification for encouraging the attitude that mistakes are praiseworthy. Yet, all too often this is precisely what happens and students are left with the mistaken idea that hamming it up or clowning around in front of an audience is the substance of the art of acting.

Another mistake that many students and teachers make is to overstress the similarities between the art of acting and the roles each individual plays in everyday life. The underlying rationale for this approach is that elementary and junior high age students generally feel more comfortable and learn more readily when theater is treated as an extension of their normal day-to-day activities. Although this approach gives students many of their first misconceptions about the nature of acting and theater, it is widely used because it is the easiest way for an instructor to introduce basic role-playing and imagination exercises.

Despite some slight similarities in method, the techniques outlined in this book are based on the opposite assumption. Theater does imitate life. Even to a child this point is obvious and there is simply no need to belabor it. Something that is not obvious and needs to be taught to most students is a knowledge of the ways in which acting and day to day life *differ*. The intention of this book is to show theater teachers some ways in which their students can be taught to isolate, identify, and practice some of these differences.

The book provides a series of ideas and exercises that can be used to fit a variety of different needs, philosophies and personalities. Naturally, the structuring of a complete acting curriculum for seven to fourteen year olds should be the province of the individual teacher and is dependent, to a certain extent, on the ages and levels of development of the students involved. No one method can serve everyone. However, if teachers can avoid discussing the goals of their theater units in terms of simple looking and high sounding but ultimately impenetrable jargon—such as *spontaneous, creative, free, imaginative*—and concentrate on the teaching of acting skills, they are sure to provide a valuable and constructive educational experience for their students. Certainly, the teaching of acting skills and techniques is at least as valuable as the myopically visionary emphasis on *creativity* that so often prevails.

2

An Introductory Acting Curriculum

Children's theater is one of the court jesters of elementary education. Almost everyone enjoys it but few people take it seriously. Part of the problem is that the terms *children's theater* and *creative drama* are used to refer to an incredibly wide and ill-defined range of experiences, attitudes, lessons, and activities. These vary from simple games and exercises that have something to do with role-playing to fully staged theater productions. The common use of the words *theater* and *drama* to refer to any activity that seems to involve role-playing, participation, or involvement on the part of the students leads students to believe that they are studying theater, drama, or acting when, in fact, they are not.

The structured lessons in this chapter involve students in six elementary principles of *acting:* imagination, concentration, observation, characterization, improvisation, and rhythm. It is designed to fit a schedule of three one hour classes a week for twelve weeks. The lessons are suitable introductory material for students in grades three through seven.

All of the exercises are performance oriented. That is, the students are always either actually working in front of other students and the teacher or preparing to work in front of them. The presence of this audience is a strong motivating factor in achieving the four major goals of the entire program.

First, each child can develop the confidence to perform in front of others, without inhibitions or fear. Second, each student can learn that acting is not showing off. Instead, it is a skill involving the recreation of believable characters and situations, plus the ability to *communicate* thoughts and feelings to others. Third, each student can learn to *control* his or her characterization as well as the dramatic situation in order to build a sequence of events that has a discernible beginning, middle and end. Finally, the students can develop a strong sense of cooperation and teamwork. They can learn how to work together in order to keep the action moving along smoothly.

Imagination

1. *Dramatic imaginings*. Most children between seven and twelve do not have to be "taught" to pretend or imagine. However, they often do need training in how to communicate their imaginings to others.

In order to develop an awareness of this kind of communication, I ask my students to create a number of imaginary situations that involve elementary pantomime and role-playing. This kind of experience can be made more vivid by asking the students a number of goal directed questions.

Such questions are in no way tests or value judgments. They are meant to help the students clarify the details of each imaginary situation. Using your own judgment, ask questions during and after the students perform. The students need not answer the questions out loud. Instead, they use them to enliven and clarify the *performance* of each situation.

The following are three sample situations that you could ask your students to pantomime, along with some questions you might ask them.

Walking a tightrope. How high up are you? Is there a safety net? Is this your first time on a tightrope? How tightly is the rope strung? Are you indoors or outdoors? If you are outdoors, is there any wind? Are you afraid? How narrow is the rope? How easy is it to keep your balance?

Walking through tall grass. How tall is the grass? Is it wet or dry? Are there animals or insects in the grass? How thick is it? Are you trying to find someone? Are you trying to escape from someone?

Walking through mud. Is the mud warm or cold? How deep is it? Do you have shoes on? Are you enjoying walking through the mud or do you want to get out of it?

2. *Mock games*. Imaginary group games help teach your students how to communicate with the other members of a theatrical group. Begin with something simple like two people playing catch with an imaginary ball or frisbee. Later on, you can work up to something as complicated as a

The teacher should be actively involved in the exercises. In this case, the teacher demonstrates *walking a tightrope* while some students watch.

Following the teacher's example, a student takes her first, difficult steps along the imaginary tightrope.

Students and teacher have a good time playing a mock game of dodge ball.

Despite the fact that no ball is used, students quickly develop a precise sense of where the ball is and how fast it is going.

complete game of baseball in which all of the props, including the ball and bat, are imaginary.

Appropriate goal directed questions might include: Does everyone know who has the ball? Is everyone playing with the same size ball? When the ball is thrown or hit, does everyone know in what direction and how fast it is going?

During these games, let the students talk to one another if they wish. But be sure to discourage them from narrating or describing rather than playing or performing the action of the games. For example, they should *not* say, "Johnny, I'm going to throw this at you. It's going to be a fast ball. Oops! I threw it over your head. No, it's not there."

3. *Small group involvement*. Without scenery or properties, one student performs a simple activity such as sweeping a kitchen floor, making beds in the bedroom, or dusting furniture in the living room. The specific details of the situation are not announced in advance to the class. As soon as another student recognizes what the performer is doing, he or she joins in the activity helping the student sweep, bringing a dustpan, emptying the dustpan. This exercise fosters basic cooperation and communication skills among the performers.

Some sample goal directed questions include: How did the original performer show that he or she was in a specific place (e.g., a living room or a kitchen)? How precise was his or her original activity? How well did the two students cooperate in the original activity?

4. *Story pantomimes*. In this exercise, individual students pantomime their interpretations of a story as it is being told. Although the complexity of the narratives can vary slightly according to the age and sophistication of your students, keep them simple and clear. Be sure each depicts a progression of emotionally charged actions.

Seated on a stool, the teacher narrates a story pantomine while the student acts it out. "You are walking home after having stayed late at school. The sun has gone down and it's cold and dark . . . ."

"You take a detour through some woods and you suddenly realize that it's completely dark. You can't see the way, so you sit down by a tree and try to calm yourself . . . ."

For example: "You are walking home after having stayed late at school. The sun has gone down, and it's cold and dark. But you're not in a hurry because you have a bad report card that you don't want to show to your parents. You take a detour through some woods and you suddenly realize that it's completely dark. You can't see the way, so you sit down by a tree and try to calm yourself. You look around and see a faint light in the distance. Carefully, you pick your way through the woods using the light as a marker. You're out of the woods, and you start to run towards the light. It's the house of a friend. You're safe!"

Story pantomimes can and should be continued for more than one class period. Some of the factors you should consider in deciding how long to continue them are: your gifts as a storyteller, the interest of the participants, and your assessment of the extent to which the students are developing.

"You look around and see a faint light in the distance . . . ."

"Carefully, you pick your way through the woods, using the light as a marker."

"It's the house of a friend. You're safe!"

Concentration

The ability to focus all attention and energy on a specific set of goals is as important to an actor as it is to an athlete, dancer or pianist.

1. *The mirror exercise*. Students are paired and told to move together as though they were mirroring on another's actions. Their goal is to make it impossible for an observer to pick out a "follower" and "leader", *not* for one performer to imitate the other's actions.

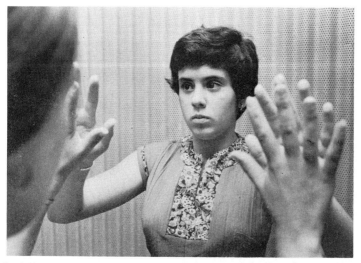

In the mirror exercise, students are paired and told to move together as though they were mirroring one another's actions.

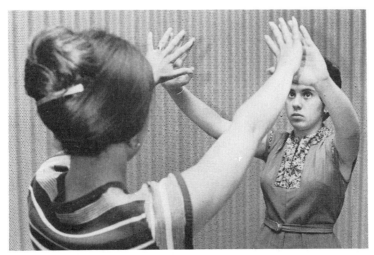
The mirror exercise requires a basic understanding of the nature of movement as well as a great deal of concentration.

This entails not only a great deal of concentration on the part of both students but also a basic understanding of the nature of movement. Does one action flow smoothly into the next? Do the actions have a rhythm? Do both participants always have a sense of what they are going to do next?

2. *The lost object.* Ask the children to imagine that they have lost a valuable object. Have them concentrate on looking for it. Ask such questions as: Is there a method to your search? When and where did you last have it? What have you done since then? Does this object mean a great deal to you? Do you want other people—or another person, in particular—to know that it is lost? Did it belong to you? Are you afraid that someone else will find it first? Have you searched everywhere?

Once again, it is best if the action is performed without words, because many students will have a perfectly natural tendency to describe rather than to show what they are feeling. This exercise can help students understand that there is more to seemingly simple actions and emotions than they may have thought.

3. *The football game.* Tell the students you will narrate a football game. If possible, bring in a recording of someone announcing an actual game. Have each person in the class choose a side before you begin and root for one of the teams while the game is narrated. After the narration, ask: Were you really pleased or were you only trying to *show* that you were pleased? Were you really disappointed or were you only trying to show that you were disappointed? Did you react only to the action of the game or did you express your feelings before or after some of the plays, too? Did you react to the people around you?

4. *The arithmetic problem*. Give one student a simple arithmetic problem to solve in his or her head. Have the other students try to distract the one who is "it" without using physical force. Can he or she find the solution?

In a related exercise, a student tries to make a paper airplane while the others do something distracting. Undoubtedly, you will think of other examples. Chapter Seven offers some concentration exercises suitable for advanced students.

Observation

It is difficult to create or recreate characters and situations without a reservoir of detailed information. The actor must be able to both *see* and *remember* specific things about people, things and events.

Do you or your students know the exact number of steps on the front porch of your home? Can the students remember what their brother or sister or mother was wearing this morning? In fact, can they, without looking, tell you what color socks they are wearing? Such questions show the students how easy it is to go through a day *seeing* an extraordinary number of things but *observing* very few of them. Here are three activities that increase the powers of observation.

1. *Observing is not staring*. Have pairs of students observe each other for one minute. Then have them face away and answer questions about one another. For example: Did the student's shirt have pockets? What color are his or her eyes?

2. *The draped tray*. Place several small objects (a thimble, a pencil, a spoon, etc.) on a tray and cover it with a cloth. Now show it for fifteen seconds or less to a student who is "it." Ask the student to try to remember what was on the tray. Since any number of objects can be used, start with a few simple ones and increase the number and complexity gradually.

3. *Pose as I pose*. Ask your students to try to duplicate your posture as you move your body into various positions. Start with a simple move such as pointing your left index finger straight up in the air. Stop and give the students a chance to imitate you. Gradually, make each pose more complicated. For instance, in the next one you might keep your left index finger straight up in the air, put your right hand on your hip and close your right eye. Ask your students to observe and imitate everything about you that they can.

Characterization

Characterization is the art of making an audience believe that an actor is someone else. The exercises below provide simplified approaches to some elements of characterization. They are particularly suitable for inexperienced actors since they are based on physical rather than analytical methods of creating a character. Additional methods will be discussed in later chapters.

1. *Imitation*. Each student is asked to go home and observe a friend or family member doing a very simple activity: eating dinner, watching television, doing homework. The student is asked to remember as many specific details about the person as possible: How did the person sit? How fast did he or she walk? Was the person happy, sad, or tired?

In class, the student then recreates his or her observations without using words. Some directed questions for the students watching this exercise might include: Exactly what was the actor's primary activity? How precise and detailed was the activity? What was the character's mood?

2. *Motivation*. Select a simple action or task and have a student or group of students perform it three different ways: A very ill person hanging up clothes, a boy being punished who has to hang up clothes, a girl who is hanging up clothes but is in a hurry to go somewhere else.

3. *What kind of person?* When students learn to concentrate on certain parts of their bodies, it helps them forget themselves and gives them the flexibility to become another character much more easily. In this first exercise, ask the students to concentrate on various parts of their faces in order to become, for example, a "nose person", a "forehead person", a "chin person". For more detail on how to do this, see the section on "Energy Points" in Chapter Five. Ask the students to show you some of the following: What different kinds of people can you make from your forehead person? How quickly can you change from being a forehead person to a nose person? How do you feel when you become a chin person? How would your chin person sweep the floor or eat soup?

a. Have a "forehead person" and a "chin person" come into a room where there is only one chair. Each wants the other to sit down on it. The students may speak if they wish.

b. A "nose person" and a "left ear" person are entering or exiting through a door. Each wants the other to go first.

c. A "left eye" person and a "right ear" person are introduced to each other for the first time.

Improvisation

By now your students are ready to make up and act out short, simple stories complete with dialogue. In the theater, improvisations are not

27

simply enjoyable role-playing exercises. Instead, they enable actors to train themselves to answer questions of motivation such as: *"How* do I cross to the desk?" or *"Why* do I say this line?" Actors must learn to create a reason or purpose for every word and action. Nothing on stage can be performed thoughtlessly.

There are many excellent theories concerning the ways in which a student can benefit through exercise and training in the techniques of dramatic improvisation. Perhaps the best known and most articulate advocates of improvisation are Viola Spolin and her son, Paul Sills. Viola Spolin was an acting teacher at Yale University for several years. She is also the author of *Improvisation for the Theatre,* which provides a complete explanation of her theories and techniques. Sills utilized and refined his mother's techniques in his widely acclaimed Story Theatre productions. Largely through the efforts of these two individuals, dramatic improvisation has long since proven itself as a means of developing certain acting skills. (1) It develops concentration and self confidence, (2) It exercises the imagination, (3) It helps formulate ensemble skills—the habit of responding to and interacting with other actors, and (4) It is a method of rehearsal that the actor can use to help provide depth and polish to characters and situations.

In order to clarify objectives and avoid confusion or uncertainty in the classroom, I have found it useful to tell students the theory behind the practice of using improvisations. I also tell them that most acting teachers introduce their students to improvisation techniques in order to prepare them for the more complicated tasks of creating characters and building scenes.

No matter how well prepared they may be in the way of exercises and explanations, many students become nervous and tense during their first full-fledged improvised scene. They cannot avoid the mistaken impression that this is their first public "performance." As a result, their efforts are often inhibited, restrained and forced rather than free and naturally flowing. Actors will often concentrate on their own characterizations and virtually ignore other players or they will concentrate on creating a situation and neglect to develop a character. They may even concentrate on both the character and the situation, forgetting important technical matters such as projection, volume and articulation.

After their first improvisational scenes, many older students will typically feel that too much has been forced upon them too quickly. They may feel that more time should have been spent in preparatory exercises, in wordless improvisations, or instructor-directed improvisations. They will very often say that it would have been more beneficial to have begun with some kind of script first because they found that most of their efforts were directed at trying to decide what to do next.

To counteract these various difficulties teachers should provide active guidance during the introductory stages of improvisation exercises. While the students are engaged in the improvisations, instructors can ask helpful questions, make suggestions or even take active roles in the scenes. Of course, as the students gain more confidence the teachers gradually withdraw their influence—leaving the students in control.

Several methods of developing improvisation skills follow. Have the students work in groups of three or more with approximately twenty minutes to prepare their scenes. Follow each performance with a session of constructive criticism. Students should be given time to improve each improvisation in subsequent rehearsal and performance sessions.

1. *Situations*. Have the students improvise brief scenes such as starting a baseball game, fixing a broken bicycle, taking care of unruly children or getting lost in the woods.

2. *Objects*. Have the students find such imagined objects as an old toy, a trunk, an old photograph album, a microscope, a mirror or an old rowboat.

3. *Conflict*. Have the students improvise characters and situations based on a central conflict. The choice of fantastic situations makes the exercise a little more enjoyable for the students and boosts their imagination by leading them away from exclusive concentration on normal, everyday events.

a. A sly pirate and a nice, but absent minded fairy godmother each want the other to sit on a chair that turns bad people good and good people bad. Although both know the powers of the chair, they each pretend to the other that they don't.

b. A cowardly escaped convict pretending to be a dentist encounters his or her first patient—a police officer.

c. Two professional braggart explorers who have found their way into the jungle both want to start home, but neither wants to admit to the other that he or she is completely lost.

Relevant questions to ask in discussions after each performance are: Did the actors listen to one another? Did the actors' words and actions *develop* from moment to moment? Did each actor develop his or her own character? Did everyone stay in character? Did the improvisations have a beginning, a middle and an end? Did the actors seem to believe in what they were doing? Did the audience?

Tempo and Rhythm in Movement and Speech

One of the most difficult lessons for student actors to learn is how to vary tempo and rhythm in movement and speech. Once mastered, students can use tempo/rhythm techniques to help create and control the moods and emotions of their characters. A complete discussion of this important topic can be found in Constantin Stanislavski's book, *Building a Character* (translated by Elizabeth R. Hapgood, Theatre Arts Books, New York, New York).

1. *Change the tempo*. Bring in a metronome and set it to a particular beat. Ask a group to act out one of its previously performed improvisations to a rhythm determined by the ticking of a metronome. Halve the beat and have the students perform their scene to the new rhythm. Then double the original beat.

It is important that the students realize that the rhythm of the scene is altered, not necessarily the speed of line delivery. Rather than speaking or moving very slowly or quickly, they should concentrate on varying the tempo of their characters and their scenes. For example, how quickly or slowly does one character respond to another's question?

Most older students find this exercise challenging and exciting. The follow up discussion should focus on the effects of tempo/rhythm on all the elements of improvisation. What happened to the characters? How did a particular moment seem to change when the tempo did? How did the change effect the general mood?

2. *Quick change*. During this exercise, vary the beat of the metronome several times during a performance of each improvisation. Did the actors really respond to the new beats? Did everyone respond at the same time? Did everyone respond to each change in the same way? How did the changes in tempo rhythm affect the improvisation?

Group Performances

Give groups of two or three students a chance to prepare either their own original improvisations or scenes from playscripts for studio performance using no costumes and minimal props. As they rehearse, encourage them to keep in mind everything they have learned thus far. Your students will both want and need a substantial amount of time to prepare. For a five to ten minute scene, two hours of rehearsal are not excessive and some older students may even want more time. Each scene or improvisation should be critiqued by the rest of the class immediately after it is performed.

Conclusion

The point of all the exercises in this chapter is to give students a practical introduction to some of the basic elements of the actor's art. Naturally, teachers should introduce the exercises to students in a manner that will stimulate and perhaps enthuse them. Much more vital is the role of the teacher in training students to observe and criticize themselves and others with intelligence and sensitivity. Teachers must have the knowledge and experience to supervise this extremely difficult learning process with patience and understanding. Without intelligent evaluation, the exercises can become simple amusements in which little is accomplished and nothing is learned.

3

Voice Training

Good speech habits can be learned early in life—especially from alert and understanding parents and teachers. It is far easier for children to learn to speak properly at the outset than it is for them to unlearn a host of bad habits and then, in effect, relearn to speak. Good speech upgrades the quality of everyday communication and is an important adjunct to reading, writing and spelling skills. Students who can't hear or say a word properly are not likely to read or spell it correctly.

The elements of good speech are: *articulation, rate/speed, volume, pronunciation, breath control, energy/relaxation,* and *variety in pitch.* Although the *elements* of good speech are the same on stage as they are in everyday life, the *standards* for stage speech are much more rigorous. Young actors must master basic speech techniques in order to be heard and understood by their audiences.

Articulation

As soon as children have learned their vowel and consonant sounds, they need to be encouraged to use them in everyday speech. They should develop the habit of completing every sound in every word before going on to the next. The word *butterfly*, for example, should not sound like *burfly*, and *skipped* should not sound like *ski*. In addition, they must learn to finish pronouncing one word before going on to the next. For instance, "Where are you going?" should not become "Wheyagoin?"

Reciting tongue twisters is probably one of the oldest and most enjoyable ways for young people to develop their skills in articulation. Here are a few old standards:

She sells sea shells by the sea shore. (Say quickly ten times in a row.)

Round and round the rugged rocks the ragged rascal ran. (Say quickly ten times in a row.)

Betty Botta bought a bit of butter and put it in her batter. "But," said she, "this batter's bitter. Perhaps the butter's bitter." So Betty Botta bought a bit of better butter and put it in her bitter batter which made her bitter batter a bit better.

Thissian Thistle, the successful thistle sifter, sifts sieves full of three thousand thistles through the thick of his thumb.

Students should be told that the care given to saying all the sounds in a tongue twister needs to be carried over into reading aloud, speaking on stage and even to speaking in everyday life.

Rate/Speed and Volume

Most normal conversation occurs between people who are only five or ten feet apart. At such close quarters, overly rapid speech and low volume usually go unnoticed. In the theater, however, distances between actors are often slightly greater than normal and distances between actors and audiences are almost always much greater than normal. Actors must make themselves heard over these greater distances without pushing or straining their voices. Students must create a convincing illusion of speaking to one another on stage. At the same time, they can never forget that they are speaking for the sake of the audience in the theater.

The term rate/speed does not refer to some mythically proper tempo. It should, instead, be thought of as a state of mind in which the actor feels free to take the time to articulate all of the sounds and to take all of the pauses. The all too common practice of a director sitting in the back of the rehearsal room and loudly, rapidly and rhythmically clapping his or her hands while urging the actors to "Speed it up. Speed it up. Speed it up" has no relationship to rate/speed.

Volume and rate/speed are closely related elements. In fact, overly rapid rate/speed is often incorrectly diagnosed as insufficient volume, and students who are already virtually yelling are told to "speak up."

Anyone who has ever spoken or called to someone standing more than one hundred and fifty feet away already knows about the relationship between volume and rate/speed. The person's volume increases in accordance with the distance to be covered and certain consonant and vowel sounds must become drawn out. For example, when spoken over a long distance, "Johnny, where are you?" becomes "Joohnneee wheere aaare youu?" If the sentence is spoken too quickly it will not be understood by the listeners no matter how closely they are standing or how loudly it is said.

On stage, the long distances between speaker and listener also call for an increase in volume coupled with a slight elongation of certain vowel and consonant sounds. This technique will be much more effective than having the actors yell to the back of the auditorium.

You can help students develop control over rate/speed and volume by involving them in exercises that force them to speak across comparatively large distances. Normal oral reading exercises successfully meet this requirement when the readers stand in front of the class and try to speak—without shouting or yelling—so that everyone in the room can hear them.

Teachers can also help their students by pointing out the oral as well as the grammatical significance of punctuation marks. Commas, periods, question marks, exclamation points and so on signify vastly different types of pauses and inflections. A pause taken too quickly is not a pause. An inflection spoken too rapidly will not be understood.

If the students are in the process of rehearsing a scene, take them into a larger room or outside and double or triple the distances between them. This exercise is effective only if the actors already know their blocking. They must try to say their lines *to* one another and tell each other when they cannot hear.

Pronunciation

Correct pronunciation involves two separate elements. First, actors' speech should be free of affectation and regional dialects. By and large, this is an advanced level problem. The second element, in which training can begin quite early, is the proper pronunciation of words. Younger children should simply be corrected whenever they mispronounce a word. Older students should be encouraged to develop the habit of referring to a dictionary for the correct pronunciation of those words about which they are uncertain.

Singing is the best and most useful all-around exercise for the voice.

Breath Control

Actors need to control the processes of inhalation and exhalation if they are to speak effectively on stage. This will allow them to vary the length and vocal quality of their phrases without having to strain or gasp for air. There are a large number of exercises which help develop breath control. Unquestionably, the best and most enjoyable of them is a regular program of group or choral singing under the leadership of a qualified instructor. In fact, singing is the best and most useful all-around exercise for the voice.

Energy/Relaxation

The ability to maintain a balance between vocal energy and vocal relaxation is difficult for anyone to master. Misdirected vocal energy leads to an unnecessarily loud or harsh voice and can give a performer a sore throat. With too much relaxation, an actor's words become difficult to understand and his or her voice becomes inexpressive.

A common cause for misplaced vocal energy is that fledgling actors frequently use unnaturally high, low or harsh voices. Young actors often believe that creating a character means "changing the voice." Helping them to learn other ways of creating characters such as those suggested in Chapter Five will go a long way toward solving many of their vocal problems. The best activity for practicing energy/relaxation is, once

35

again, singing. The simple direction "Don't sing—but relax and speak as *though* you were singing," will often work extremely well.

Variety in Pitch and Phrasing

Some students have no apparent problem speaking or reading aloud with both variety of expression and animation. Others speak their lines in a virtual monotone, unconsciously dividing their parts into phrases of equal duration and inflecting all their phrases in the same way.

Students need to learn that any word or phrase can be given a variety of different meanings according to the ways in which the actor inflects the lines. A good way to introduce preschool and primary grade children to this concept is to have them pretend that they are animals in specific situations. For example, they can be cats looking for something to eat, lost sheep trying to find their way home or cows searching for a calf that has wandered away. Since they are animals they don't use words. Instead, they speak in animal language—"meow" for cats, "baa" for sheep, "moo" for cows, and so on. Free of the problems involved in having to make up and speak lines, the children will inflect their voices in order to help create the imaginary situations. Once the idea has been introduced to children, it will frequently become a part of their normal play activity. In these early stages, there is no need for further structure or supervision.

For seven and eight year olds, an enjoyable way to further develop vocal expressiveness is a nonsense sound conversation. In this exercise, the teacher provides a simple, imaginary situation. Based upon it, students improvise a "conversation" by repeating a single nonsense syllable such as *ta* or long *a*. For example, student #1 has just found a huge frog in the corner of a garden and wants student #2 to come and look at it. The result might be something like this:

> Student #1: "A." (Come here.)
> Student #2: "A?" (Why?)
> Student #1: "A!" (Come here!)
> Student #2: "A?" (What do you want?!)
> Student #1: "A!" (Please, come here!)
> Student #2: "A!" (Wow, that's really something!)

Students usually like this exercise and, when left to their own devices, can develop surprisingly long and complicated situations.

For students aged nine and older, variety in pitch and phrasing can be developed still further. Individual students are asked to repeat a single line. Each time the student says the line, he or she *imagines* a different situation that is suggested by the teacher.

"Don't go outside." (Said by a girl to her younger brother. He wants to go outside but it is too cold and rainy.)

"Don't go outside." (Two friends have just quarreled. The speaker wants to coax the person who is leaving to stay inside and play.)

"Don't go outside." (Said by a boy to his two year old sister who is running to the front door. The boy knows there is a vicious dog just outside the door. If his sister goes outside, she may be bitten.)

"Don't go outside?" (A girl has just been told not to go outside by her father. She wants to know why.)

This exercise can, of course, be performed using any number of different phrases and imagined situations. Some students will have an extraordinary aptitude for reading meaning and emotion into their lines. Others will have to be guided through the various interpretations of each phrase with enormous patience and care. The point is for them to vividly imagine themselves as specific characters in each particular situation. For lines to be spoken with both precision and variety, a performer's dramatic imagination must constantly be at work.

Projection

The ability to combine and use all of the elements discussed in this chapter in order to communicate with an audience is called *projection*. *Volume* and *projection* are not the same thing. No matter how loudly they are spoken, lines that are rushed, poorly phrased, badly articulated or spoken without thought and feeling will not be understood by an audience.

Most experts agree that it takes about two years of work to develop a good speaking voice. The exercises in this chapter are only a beginning. Two of the best books for further information on the subject are *The Use and Training of the Human Voice* by Arthur Lessac and Kristin Linklater's *Freeing the Natural Voice*.

Good speech is one of the basics of the actor's art. Almost all students can speak, but very few of them can speak well enough to make themselves understood on stage. It is the responsibility of teacher/directors to deal with this problem in ways that are imaginative, disciplined and well informed.

4

Developing a Visual Sense for Stage Movement

Audiences won't listen to a play if they aren't watching it. Even in plays with elaborate scenery and costumes, the actors' movements are the visual substance of the drama. The best teacher/directors know this and constantly strive to transform what they read in a printed script into an expressive, constantly moving stage picture.

Many inexperienced director/teachers think that the problems involved in blocking a play (planning the actors' movements) are either unimportant or will more or less take care of themselves. Others have a slightly different, but no less inaccurate belief. Forgetting that theater is not simply an imitation of everyday life, they are convinced that the director need only help the actors move as though the stage actions were a series of real-life situations. However, the purpose of stage blocking is to help actors express and audiences to understand and appreciate the ideas, moods and relationships that are stated or implied in a given script. As such, stage movement must always be far more expressive, precise and interesting to watch than its everyday counterpart.

Fortunately, there are some basic guidelines for understanding and using blocking techniques. First, the director must know how to *focus* the audience's attention so that it is always looking in the right place at the right time. The good director is like a good magician. He or she constantly uses movement to direct the audience's attention towards or away from specific onstage actions. Second, each important movement of the play must always be visible to the audience. For example, if a character's facial expression is particularly significant at a given moment, it might be wise to block her into a downstage cross so that as she moves her face can be seen by the audience. Third, *clarity* and *economy* of movement are also vital. This means that all movement must be clear and expressive in ways that help the actors as well as the audience to understand and appreciate the characters and their situations. There is no place for extraneous movement—movement that expresses nothing about the characters or the play. Fourth, every piece of blocking must be *suitable* to the play and the characters. It would probably not be suitable, for example, to show Cinderella's stepmother dribbling a basketball at the Prince's grand ball. Fifth, there is the problem of *timing*. Timing is not quite so dependent on an actor's instincts as many inexperienced director/teachers believe. Just as certain athletic treams can learn to time a difficult and complicated series of maneuvers simply by counting out when they are supposed to go where, so actors can and should be taught to do the same. In fact, the ability to count out a complicated series of moves is at least as important as a rehearsal technique as it is an element of athletic training. Finally, the director must strive to make the moving stage picture aesthetically pleasing to watch.

Even directors who understand that blocking is a time consuming and complex art are often plagued by genuine philosophical problems. "Wouldn't it be better," they frequently ask, "to encourage students to develop their own blocking during the rehearsal period?" The question is a good one and can best be answered by asking some questions about the rehearsal process.

Do the students come to early rehearsals with an acceptable understanding of how to go about creating their roles or developing their relationships with the other characters in the play? If, as is most often the case, they do not, then the director must facilitate this understanding through the use of preplanned, expressive blocking. Blocking patterns of the type explained later in this chapter are particularly useful for this purpose.

Can the students distinguish movement that imitates real life from stage blocking that expresses mood and meaning to an audience? If they can't, then the director's blocking is an absolute necessity. Students cannot come up with their own ideas of how their characters should move until they understand some of the purposes and techniques of stage movement.

Do the actors have a moment to moment understanding of their function on the stage from an audience's point of view? Are they able to coordinate their own blocking in the light of a total vision of the play? Frankly, even the most professional of actors often need and want a director's help in these matters. And it is the director's blocking plan that can be the most important key to a well-planned and organized vision of a play. Naturally, during rehearsals, as the performers come to understand more and more about the play and their roles, they should be encouraged to contribute their own ideas which may well add to or even change the director's original plans. Even in this case, the final responsibility for blocking the play rests with the director.

Blocking is largely a visual art and what follows is a series of exercises which, when properly used, will help develop a prospective director's visual sense. Each pattern can be easily demonstrated and explained to students aged twelve and older.

I usually begin by explaining the functions of stage blocking. Then, I diagram a movement pattern on the blackboard, explaining how (but not why) each character is supposed to move. At this point, I ask students to walk through the pattern while improvising a short situation based upon the movement. Different students will usually come up with different uses, situations and motivations for each movement. Although this variety should be encouraged, it is important that there be no deviation from the given movement pattern. After working in this way for a class period or two, I then ask the students to create and name a few of their own patterns by diagramming them on paper. Individuals are selected to draw their best patterns on the blackboard and other students are encouraged to improvise motivations and situations based on these patterns.

If no one can figure out a use for a particular pattern, then the student who created it must show at least one way in which it can be performed. Afterwards, the class can discuss how effective the pattern actually was. Were there turns or steps that seemed to serve no purpose? Did the audience look in the right place at the right time? Were all the important relationships or facial expressions clearly visible to the audience? Was the movement pleasing to watch? Was it expressive? You and your students will think of other appropriate questions and will undoubtedly be able to think of other names and different uses for the patterns that are diagrammed and explained on the following pages.

1. SIMUL-SCRATCH

Two or three people who are standing or sitting in the same fashion scratch their heads, cross their legs, or perform some other action or sequence of actions in unison. This is a good comedy bit.

When four or more people perform a simul-scratch, they can easily be made to appear chillingly regimented or robotized.

Points to note: (1) A series of simultaneous actions performed on stage represents an extremely strong visual statement. (2) All actors must know precisely how, when, and in what order the actions are performed.

Two people cross a few steps away from each other, stop for a moment, cross away another one or two steps, and then stop again. This blocking pattern can show two people who have something to say to one another, but cannot look at each other to say it. When the two people move and stop in unison, the movement will tend to appear comic. When they move one at a time, the pattern will tend to be more useful in serious scenes.

Point to note: Actors do not need to face or move toward one another in order to establish a relationship.

2. THE "HOW CAN I TELL YOU?" THINGO

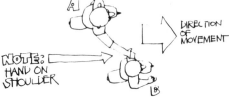

Two people cross the stage. A has his hand on B's shoulder. B walks slightly ahead of A so that the audience can easily see both characters. The move could be used to help show that A is giving B some friendly advice or perhaps A has just been forced to fire B and is politely but firmly ushering him toward the door.

Point to note: In real life, the characters would probably walk side by side. The positions have been altered so that both characters are visible to the audience for the entire length of the cross.

4. CIRCULAR STAND OFF

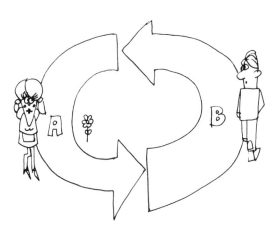

Two characters stand about seven feet apart, look at each other over their shoulders, and circle in the same direction. Perhaps they are sizing one another up prior to a fight, or maybe A is a bold girl and B is a shy boy.

Point to note: This pattern can be explained and performed with comparative ease, even by inexperienced actors. Nonetheless, it can be used in any number of ways.

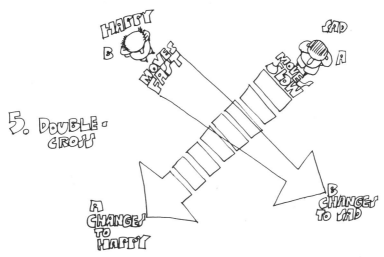

A crosses down right. Then B crosses down left, passing behind A. This kind of pattern might be used to help express the idea that two characters on opposite sides of an issue are suddenly persuaded to adopt the other's point of view.

Points to note: (1) This pattern is a simple yet imaginative way to help express the meaning of an apparently static moment in a play. (2) Although it would probably never occur in real life, it is still expressive and useful on stage. (3) It will focus the audience's attention on each speaker in turn.

A crosses directly toward B, backing B into a wall or a piece of furniture. At the last moment, B sidles away and escapes. It is possible that A is deliberately bullying B. It is also possible that A merely approaches B in a normal fashion, but that B feels guilty or ashamed about something.

Point to note: An actor who backs up on stage makes a very strong statement about his character and/or the situation. Actors should never back up on stage unless they know exactly why they are doing so, and are sure that they will be safe. It is all too easy to fall off a platform or to trip over a piece of furniture while moving backward.

WALK · SIT

Someone walks quickly to a chair and then sits down abruptly. The quick sit might indicate that the character has just received some kind of surprise or shock. It could also be used to help show that a character is just being stubborn.

Point to note: The audience's attention is focused on the character undergoing a change in thought or mood. For this reason, he or she should face the audience during the cross.

8. SLO SIT RICOCHET

SLOWLY SIT · JUMPS UP

The character sits slowly, thinks a moment, then jumps up quickly and faces the audience. The movement can indicate that he is undergoing an emotional change. It might also be used to show that he is coming up with a new idea or plan of action.

Point to note: This move shows a double change in emotions; one, when the character sits, and a second when he stands. If the character concludes by facing downstage, the audience will be ready to focus on what he is going to do next. On the other hand, if this character concludes by facing upstage, the audience will be prepared to shift their attention to another part of the stage.

A moves in a semicircular pattern behind the seated *B*. *A* could be trying to draw attention to himself while *B* is busy reading a magazine. Another possibility is that military officer, *A*, struts behind political prisoner, *B*, while questioning him.

Point to note: The standing figure's movement pattern and physical relationship to the seated character can make an apparently neutral series of questions seem menacing. Try this pattern with the standing character asking: "What is your name?" "Where do you live?" "What do you do for a living?" Notice how the reactions of both characters are almost always visible to the audience.

Two people are arguing. A moves about the stage turning on the light, opening the window, closing a door, and so forth. After each action, *B* follows and turns off the light, closes the window, opens the door, etc.

Point to note: The audience's attention will shift back and forth between the characters. In addition, audiences will tend to focus on the character who is performing a deliberate action such as opening (or closing) the window.

11. SIMUL- TURN + FACE AWAY

After a heated discussion, two characters turn so that their backs are toward one another. Possibly, they are indicating that neither of them has anything further to say.

Point to note: Because they both move at the same time, the effect will usually be slightly comic. This kind of move is a useful way to lighten the effect of a comic argument.

12. SIMUL- TURN + FACE IN

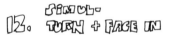

The two characters feel silly about their behavior and turn to face one another in an attempt to make up.

Point to note: Actors should hardly ever deliver lines while standing face to face. Instead, each should take a quarter turn toward the audience. This technique, called "cheating," or "facing out," allows the audience a clear view of the actors' faces.

The quarrel resumes when *A* says something in anger. *B* turns away in disgust, and then *A* turns away. (Experiment and notice the differences between this and the Simul-Turn and Face Away.)

Point to note: This pattern helps convey a visual impression of a realistic argument. If the actors were to move simultaneously, as opposed to consecutively, the director and actors could more easily create a stylized, slightly comic effect.

14. SIMUL-STAND

Two characters rise from a sitting position in unison. The movement could be used to show agreement between the characters. They reach agreement and rise to embark on a shared course of action. The same movement could, of course, also be used to help show disagreement. The characters have reached the climax of an argument and rise to challenge one another.

Point to note: This move alerts the audience that something is just about to happen. Audiences must be *led* to look in the right places at the right times.

Two characters enter from opposite sides of the stage. They walk backward and search the area with extreme caution. When they are about ten feet apart, they begin to move in a large circle with their backs facing one another. They start to move straight backward, and then bump into one another. This bit has been performed with innumerable variations. Nonetheless, when properly done, it is still funny.

Point to note: Because no audience will ever believe that this kind of move would occur naturally, it lends itself to a peculiar type of comic style. Audiences tend to derive pleasure from the degree of precision and intricacy with which the pattern is performed.

Countering is a common stage movement in which A moves out from behind B into a position where he or she can be seen by the audience.

Point to note: This is an exceedingly important basic stage movement that all actors should instinctively perform whenever they are unintentionally blocked from the audience's view by another actor.

48

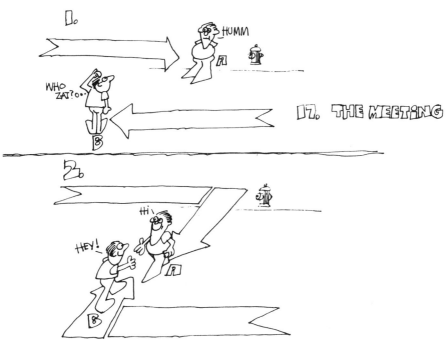

A and B cross the stage in opposite directions. They go past one another, recognize one another, then turn and cross to the center where they meet to shake hands, embrace, confront one another, or whatever.

Point to note: Pay particular attention to the points where the characters change direction and move toward one another. The change in direction should signal a transition in thought or mood. Experiment with altering the speeds of all the crosses, using the turns as the basic points of transition. For example, A moves quickly left, pauses, snaps his fingers, and then moves slowly down left; B moves slowly right, then quickly turns and *runs* up to meet A.

18. I HAVE A PLAN

A and B cross to one another from opposite directions. One puts his arm around the other's shoulders, and then they walk downstage (toward the audience) a few steps, and stop. They have a plan in the works and what they are saying is important to the audience.

Point to note: The audience is being "set up" to overhear a conversation. It had better be important.

19. HERE'S WHAT WE DO:

A and B cross to one another from opposite directions. One puts his arm around the other, and then they walk upstage (away from the audience) a few steps. They have a plan in the works but what they say is not meant to be overheard by the other characters in the play or by the audience.

Point to note: Although this upstage cross is almost as eyecatching as the preceding pattern, it tends to draw the characters out of the audience's direct focus. The audience is now ready to shift its attention to another part of the stage.

20. CLOSING IN

A moves slowly and quietly down left to an upstage side of B. B does not see or hear A. A may have a pleasant surprise for B. On the other hand, A could be about to attack B.

Point to note: Most moves on stage are neither directly upstage nor directly downstage, but diagonal or curved. In all crosses, the direction in which the characters are *facing* is very important. You can check this by having A cross diagonally upstage with B standing and facing him at the upstage end of his cross.

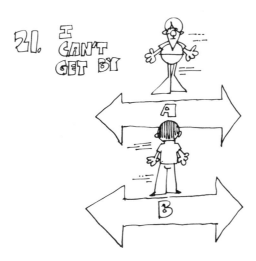

21. I CAN'T GET BY

A and B are trying to get by one another. Simultaneously, they step left a step or two and then right a step or two. The move is a useful way to show an awkward or accidental meeting between two people.

If one character, let us say it is A, moves a little bit sooner than the other, the movement may also signify that A is in a position of greater strength than B and does not want to let B get by.

Point to note: This pattern often occurs in everyday life. Directors and actors can learn a great deal by observing how people move in real life and then adapting the real life moves for stage use.

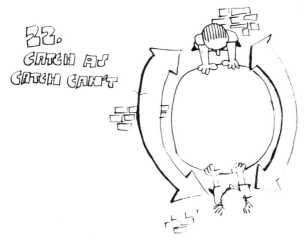

22. CATCH AS CATCH CAN'T

Two characters are standing on opposite sides of a table. One chases the other around the table to the right but cannot catch him (or her). They pause and talk for a moment or two and then resume the chase by circling around the table to the left.

Point to note: This pattern can only be repeated for a short time before the audience will begin to tire of it.

Two characters pace the floor in opposite directions trying to find a solution to a shared problem. Suddenly, each of them gets an idea. At the same moment, they whirl to face each other and then either tell one another their thoughts or reject what they were going to say and continue pacing.

Point to note: The fact that characters move in opposite directions gives the audience a clear view of both of them. It also serves to balance the stage picture.

An object of interest to two characters—e.g., a telephone—sits on a table. Both characters say that they are not interested in it, and walk away from it or otherwise pretend to ignore it. At a given moment—e.g.,the telephone rings—they rush to the object, thus revealing their true feelings.

Point to note: The manner in which the characters walk away and return can be specifically blocked to help convey different impressions about each of them.

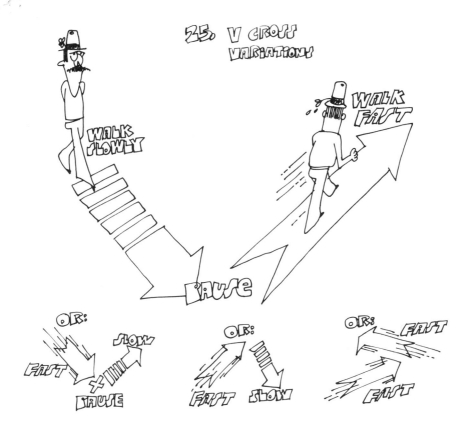

25. V CROSS VARIATIONS

WALK SLOWLY

WALK FAST

PAUSE

OR: FAST X SLOW PAUSE

OR: FAST SLOW

OR: FAST FAST

In all V crosses, the character moves to a point, pauses for an instant or two, and then moves away so that the pattern traced on the floor resembles a V. The apex of the V can be upstage, downstage or to stage left or right. In any case, a V cross can be an excellent way to help an actor portray and an audience to understand a change (or transition) in the character's mood or intention.

Point to note: V crosses are so effective in helping performers understand transitions that they can be used in rehearsals even when you have no intention of keeping the cross in the final blocking.

Look at the large illustration. As the character slowly crosses down, perhaps he is thinking. Then he pauses and crosses quickly up to show that his decision is made and his resolve is firm. The fact that he ends up with his back to the audience may mean that he is attempting to conceal his emotions from other characters on stage. Experiment with the other three V crosses that are illustrated and see what you can come up with.

A enters through a door from offstage. Simultaneously, B crosses to the door from center stage. They meet in the doorway. B backs away one or two steps while A crosses a few steps into the room. A nods and B exits. This movement may be used to show that A has a higher business or social status than B. B is a private, A a general. A is a president, B a vice-president, and so forth.

Point to note: Note how the characters move so that they do not block one another from the audience's view.

B crosses toward A, who is seated in a chair. B then pauses by the side of the chair. In the meantime, A rises and moves away from the chair, allowing B to sit. Perhaps A is a court page pretending to be king and B is the king. You can probably think of other appropriate uses.

Point to note: B is clearly the dominant character, but the pattern provides the time for the audience to see A's reaction before rising. A good deal of experimentation with this pattern can be based on varying the lengths of B's pause and A's reaction. It is an excellent pattern with which to illustrate the value of timing.

78. THE LOLLIPOP APPRAISAL

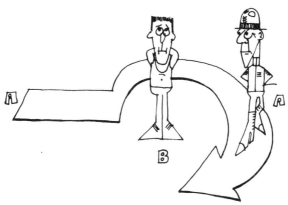

A enters and circles the stationary B. Perhaps A is gauging B's looks or intelligence. A could be a sergeant sizing up a raw recruit, or a fairy godmother examining a new ball gown that she has just created for B.

Point to note: A will tend to grab the audience's attention until he or she walks in front of B and begins to cross upstage. At this point, assuming that A always looks at B, the audience will tend to focus on B.

79. THE SHY SIDLE

A moves a few steps downstage, then pauses, then sidles across the stage a step or two, pauses again, and finally loops in toward the stationary B. Perhaps A wants to meet B but is extremely shy.

Point to note: On stage, even an apparently indecisive action has to be blocked with clarity and precision.

An absent-minded person heads for a destination, changes direction, stops for a moment, then remembers where he was headed and continues along the original path.

Point to note: The pause in the movement should be used to help motivate the change in direction.

31. THE SIMUL-SQUEEZE PLAY

At the same moment, A crosses to the right and B crosses to the left of the stationary C. Perhaps they are trying to persuade or to force C to do something. Maybe they are asking C to do them a favor.

Point to note: Despite the fact that A and B are moving, the audience will tend to focus their attention on C.

A crosses up and around to the opposite side of B. Perhaps A, in a roundabout way, is trying to explain a difficult point to the stationary B.

Conclusion

Most playgoers are more attuned to the techniques of playwriting than they are to the visual methods and tricks of directing. As a result, even habitual theatergoers are often unaware of the extent to which they have been affected by the blocking of a play.

The suggestions offered here provide a basic idea of what blocking patterns are and how they can be used. They are meant to stimulate you and your students to think visually. The early stages of blocking can be thought of as the linking together of small patterns into ones that are longer and more complicated.

There is, of course, a great deal more to the art of blocking than creating patterns. Further information will be found in any textbook on the art of directing. *Theatrical Direction: The Basic Techniques*, by David Welker; *The Craft of Play Directing*, by Curtis Canfield, and *Creating Theater: The Art of Theatrical Directing*, by August Staub, are particularly useful.

In any event, once you have begun to develop a visual sense, you may want to learn more about the art of blocking. For this, there are no substitutes for reading, intelligent discussion, and frequent practice.

5

Characterization: Three Rehearsal Processes

There is no shortage of systems and methods that can be used to help a young performer develop and create a character. Nonetheless, those of us who teach acting are always on the lookout for ideas that can help to guide and stimulate a beginner through the complicated processes of creating a character. There are, of course, no substitutes for training, experience, concentration, intelligent textual analysis, and sound theater sense. On the other hand, there are techniques which are relatively easy for the young and/or inexperienced actors to understand that can provide them with strong foundations upon which they can begin to build.

It is fine for professional acting teachers to talk about training actors for two or three years before letting them tackle their first roles, but for many of us that kind of ideal has little reference to our day-to-day problems. As often as not, an actor's first experience with theater occurs as he or she prepares for a major part in a school play. Perhaps we could all agree that that is not the way it should be, but for many of us—like it or not—that is the way it is.

Faced with four to six week production deadlines and other rehearsal pressures, teacher/directors need some efficient and reliable techniques that can, be used *in the process of rehearsal* to help novice actors create stageworthy characters. The *energy points, rehearsal units* and *hand exercises* described in the following pages are all designed to meet this common need.

Energy Points

By learning to use *energy points*, inexperienced actors can be taught to discipline their powers of concentration into creative and properly theatrical channels. The advantages of this method are twofold. One, it can easily be explained—even to seven and eight year olds—and two, it can be used to start novice actors on their way towards the creation of characters at the very outset of rehearsals. (For a suggestion on how to use energy points as a classroom exercise, see Chapter Two.)

Actors are taught to concentrate on certain parts of their faces so that they can become, for example, "nose people," "chin people," or "forehead people." Most students quickly discover that by concentrating on their chins they will begin to feel differently about themselves. They may begin to feel more assertive, proud, or combative—or they may find that their walks, mannerisms and line readings begin to take on the characteristics of the "chin people" that they have created. By the same token, the "nose person," depending on how the actor works, may become curious, aloof, or arrogant. The "forehead person" may become elegant, intellectual, domineering and so forth.

These specific associations are given only as examples of what *may* occur. There is no precise way to predict what actors will think of when

By learning to use energy points, inexperienced actors can be taught to discipline their powers of concentration into creative and properly theatrical channels.

59

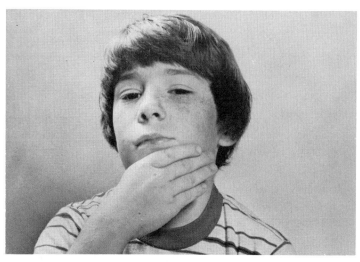

If the actors are having trouble concentrating on any particular point on their faces, it is often helpful for them to lightly massage that point while trying to concentrate on it.

they begin to concentrate on a particular energy point. It is clear, however, that the method helps young performers focus their physical and psychological energies in the right directions. Using this technique, young or inexperienced students can be led to portray moods and meanings that they might not be able to discuss.

When training actors to become conscious of energy points, I usually begin with those mentioned above: nose, forehead, and chin. At first, the students are asked to walk slowly around the room as "nose" people. Once they begin to develop an internal understanding of what it feels like to be "nose" people, they are encouraged to examine objects in the room and talk to one another as "nose" characters. Then we move on to "chin" and "forehead" people. If the actors are having trouble concentrating on any particular point on their faces, it is often helpful for them to lightly massage that point while trying to concentrate on it. Again, no one point has any clearly defined meaning. The "forehead person" may become an intellectual or a lout or one of a number of other things. The actors may want to experiment with how many different "forehead people" they can create or they may choose one energy point "character" and then start to make it as detailed as possible. Often, after only an hour or so of practice, a group of actors will have a surprisingly well-developed sense of how to isolate and use energy points. A remarkable flexibility can be developed simply by encouraging the actors to have fun with their new skills. One useful exercise is to call out "nose," "chin," or "forehead" in rapid succession as the actors walk about the rehearsal room or stage.

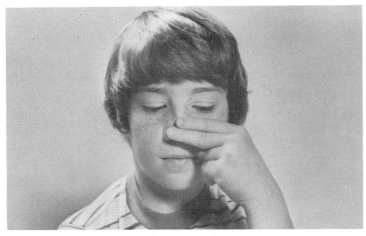

A student concentrates on his nose . . . .

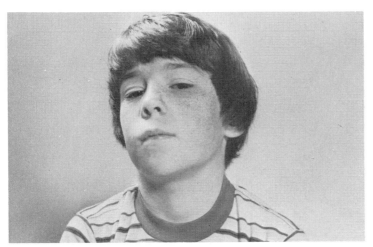

. . . and begins to feel like the "nose person" that he has created.

After work has been completed on the first three energy points, an awareness of others should be developed. The right side of the nose, the left eyebrow, the upper lip, the lower lip, the right ear lobe, the left cheek bone and the left eye are some obvious possibilities.

The perceptive and resourceful director or acting teacher will quickly discover how each student is most likely to respond to certain energy points. Instructors can and should use this knowledge to help guide the actor's processes of creating a character in ways that fit the play, the actor and the director's production concept.

At this stage, the director helps each actor choose specific energy points that are appropriate to his or her character. He then has groups of two or three actors rehearse sections of the play using the energy points

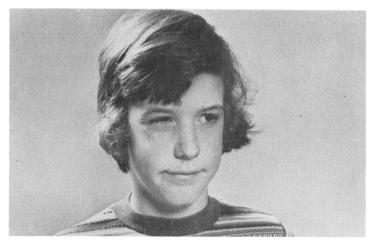

A student experiments as a "left eye person."

Under the guidance of the director/instructor, energy points can be used to help establish relationships between characters.

that have been selected. Under the guidance of the director/instructor, these energy points are used to help establish individual characters and relationships between the characters.

The manner in which this can work in rehearsal can be clarified by the following example. Recently, a twelve-year-old actor working with me on a production of *Tom Sawyer* initiated work on a very fine characterization of Injun Joe by concentrating on his eyeteeth. He claimed that this technique helped him to find and project the particular type of cruelty that suited his character. He had no foreknowledge that concentrating on his eyeteeth would have this particular effect, but a careful reading of the text in combination with a rigorous search for the proper energy points led him toward the right solution.

More advanced actors can build on this basic technique by learning to concentrate on combinations of energy points: the chin and the right eyebrow, or the lower lip and the right ear. As the students experiment with new combinations, they may be surprised to discover within themselves new or untapped emotional and psychological forces and resources. The existence of tangible, physical reference points helps each actor to both control and recall every creation. By finding new combinations of energy points, actors can develop their powers of concentration and flexibility. They can find new techniques for inspiring and creating both present and future characters.

Of course, there is no reason why actors must restrict their search for energy points to their faces and heads. However, experience has taught me that it is almost always better to leave the teaching of energy points on other parts of the body until after the students have developed sophistication with those on the face and head. Almost invariably, whenever I have begun with energy points on the body the students have tended to over-exaggerate or caricaturize whatever they were doing.

When teaching students to concentrate on energy points on their bodies, I normally tell them to imagine that there is a miniature engine that controls and drives their body located in the belly button, the breast bone, or elsewhere. This helps to avoid the common problem of the students simply forcing their stomachs out or puffing their chests up with little or no sense of what they are doing.

An almost infinite number of energy points can be found on the body which will help to develop an actor's sense of character and concentration. As is the case with developing those on the face, the actor should try single, specific energy points before attempting combinations.

The use of energy points need not be restricted to beginning actors. A surprising number of my former advanced university level acting students tell me that they still use the technique either to help create a new character or to revitalize a character that seems to be slipping away from them. The technique of using energy points may have been developed for beginners, but even talented and experienced actors continue to find it useful.

Primary Rehearsal Units

Primary rehearsal units are also extremely helpful techniques that have proved their value to a wide range of beginning, intermediate and advanced actors. Once a student has mastered these rehearsal units, they can be used to create, sustain and regulate a surprisingly wide range of theatrically valid actions and responses. Two or three of these units can be combined in a variety of ways, with results that are infinitely more complicated and subtle than might normally be expected from a novice performer.

The units that I use can be divided into two distinct types. Those of the first type are all based on emotional or physical action verbs such as fight, steal, avoid, protect and soothe. You can probably think of others as they suit your needs. I often use these particular verbs, however, because I have discovered that many student actors, with a little encouragement, can quickly develop a working emotional awareness of them.

During the first exercise, for example, an actor could be encouraged or goaded to "fight" with an old coat or towel by hitting it against the back of chair in the center of the stage or rehearsal room. The director might suggest that the chair is a hungry mountain lion who has just killed the actor's dog. Now, it has begun to stalk the actor. The towel is a stick and is the only protection the actor has. The action verbs might be *avoid* and *fight* only when cornered.

During an emotional action exercise, an actor is encouraged to "fight" with an old towel by hitting it against the back of a chair.

With a little active direction, it is astonishing how quickly the actors can commit themselves to this type of exercise. By active direction, I do not mean low-key, sideline comments. The directors must demonstrate and cajole as well as encourage. If the actor needs opposition, the director provides it. If the actor needs a victim, the director becomes one. For example the director might become the lion, snarling and trying to circle behind the actor. The goal, however, is to get the actor to work alone and with complete conviction. When the exercise works, older students typically express surprise at the intensity of their responses—at how "real" acted feelings can be.

After an initial period of emotional resettling-calming down and getting used to his or her emotional and psychological resources—the student usually asks to be allowed to try again. Clearly, the drive to improve upon past attempts is extremely important and must be encouraged. After a little more work, the teacher can suggest that the performer practice at home. Then the student is urged to come back and demonstrate what he or she has been able to accomplish. At the next session, the verb unit is practiced over and over again until the actor can create and control it with relative ease. As soon as he or she has developed a playable understanding of the unit, the actor is encouraged to sustain it for as long a time as possible. After a short while, it becomes part of the actor's emotional reservoir and he or she quickly discovers that it can be turned on or off or regulated at will.

Next, the actor should rehearse a short scene from the play while working on a specific emotional or physical action verb unit—for example, *angry* or *soothe*. In other words, the actor plays the entire scene as if he or she were angry or trying to soothe another character. After some practice, the actor redoes the same scene using an entirely different action verb unit. The real meaning of the scene does not matter at this stage. The emphasis is on developing the actor's skill in performing a specific verb unit. This technique will have to be carefully explained to most students who will not necessarily understand that the scenes are being used simply as convenient exercise material.

Once again, direction should be *positive* and *active*. Students are much more likely to go along with a teacher/director who is actively committed to the exercise than they are with one who simply criticizes an actor's performance.

Only after the actor has developed facility with two or three action verb units can the real work on interpretation of the script and characterization begin. For example, directors who want actors to play anger more convincingly may discover, as I have, that after the actor has established a successful "fight" unit, simple sideline directions such as "less fight" or "more fight" will elicit clear responses that allow the actor and director to

With one type of rehearsal unit, the actor is encouraged to imitate well-known personalities, or famous characters. This student does King Kong.

While experimenting with rehearsal units, this student came up with a fairly good imitation of Groucho Marx.

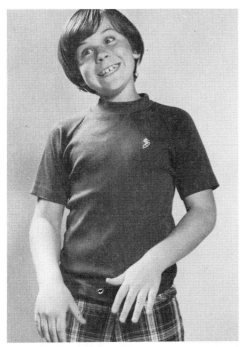

The student tries Tweety Bird. The point is for the actor to use the imitation as the first step toward the creation of a completely original character.

work more precisely with specific shades of anger than might have otherwise been possible.

With the second type of rehearsal unit, the actor is encouraged to imitate well-known personalities or famous characters: Bugs Bunny, Cookie Monster, Groucho Marx and so on. Sometimes, with a student who is obviously a good mimic, I will suggest a character. More often than not, however, I will simply ask the student if he or she does any imitations. I then try to apply what the actor can already do to the task at hand. The actor goes through an entire speech or scene while doing his or her imitation. The aim is not to create yet another imitation of Groucho Marx or Cookie Monster. Instead, the actor uses the imitation as the first step toward the creation of a completely original character. The most important part of the imitation is, in fact, the actor's commitment to and control of it. The point is to transfer the commitment and control of the imitation to the process of creating a character.

A clever director can find relationships between almost any imitation and any character. To take a deliberately outrageous example, an actress playing Goldilocks could use some elements of a Groucho Marx imitation. The curiosity and aggressiveness that are so much a part of Groucho Marx could easily be applied to Goldilocks.

I once directed a young actress who found a handle on her character, the stepmother in *Cinderella*, through the medium of a Cookie Monster imitation. Although the final characterization was nothing like Cookie Monster, the directions "more Cookie Monster" or "less Cookie Monster" established a vocabulary that she and I could use to help develop a totally new character. She learned to change her vocal patterns, her walk and so on with reference to Cookie Monster. Yet this was our secret. By the time of the first performance, no member of the audience could have recognized either an imitation or even elements of an imitation of Cookie Monster.

The idea is for the actor and director, working in concert, to create two or three strong, workable *primary rehearsal units* based on the exercises discussed. Combining two or three of them in varying amounts of intensity can produce a surprisingly large range of useful and complicated responses. When working on specific scenes, these units, once established, can function as enormously valuable regulating devices that can help form and mold precise character development and careful textual analysis.

The use of these primary units in rehearsal does not involve any complicated procedures that could divert attention and energy from work on the play. The first step is to pick the student or students who might benefit from the technique. Sometimes it will take at least a week before the director can make an adequately informed decision. The next step is to have individual working sessions with the selected actors in order to determine what units should be developed.

In order to avoid unnecessary confusion, it is important that the units be introduced one at a time. I normally schedule two or three fifteen to twenty minute sessions before the start of regular rehearsals. This length of time is quite adequate. I have found that most students are much more responsive before rehearsals than afterwards, probably because they are less tired. Lessons learned in these short pre-rehearsal sessions will be utilized in the regular rehearsals that follow so that the actor's work can be reinforced and checked. Obviously, the growth of an individual actor means nothing if it is not incorporated into the work of those with whom he must perform, and special care must be taken to make the other actors aware of any significant changes. The development of the requisite number of units should not take any longer than five or six days for any one actor, although with continuing practice each unit is bound to become more valuable as a rehearsal tool.

After the student has mastered his or her units, the director can begin approaching "problem" scenes by sitting on the sidelines and giving the actor verbal clues based upon them. Since these clues represent a highly individualized type of communication between two people, they will likely mean little or nothing to anyone other than those who were most involved with their creation—the student performer and the director. Yet, a comment such as "a little more Shirley Temple and a little less *steal*" may mean a great deal within the context of a particular actor/director relationship. A director who uses this technique will discover that the same two or three units are likely to spark different responses in different individuals.

It is essential to remember that the use of these *primary rehearsal units* is only one way in which a director can help students amplify their understanding of the actor's art. It is not a substitute for more complete training. However, the fact that it can be effectively used to help train a young and inexperienced student actor—in the process of rehearsal—makes it a useful addition to directorial technique. It is one way in which a director can help actors "energize" their performances through greater psychological awareness of and emotional commitment to their roles. More importantly, at a very early stage it fosters a kind of precision that may be difficult or impossible to achieve by other means.

Hand Exercises

Among director/teachers, perhaps no plea is more widely heard and more unsuccessfully dealt with than ". . .but what do I do with my hands?" Many inexperienced actors try to solve the problem by shoving them "out of sight", deep into their pockets or behind their backs. The hands of others droop lifelessly at their sides, occasionally twitch once or twice, and then go dead again. Still others have hands that flutter and flap in energetic patterns in no way related to the character they are trying to project.

Acting and directing texts normally don't help much. They say either that awkward hands are a sign of inexperience or uncertainty, as if everyone didn't already know that, or that the actors who have difficulty with their hands are simply not committed to their roles. Once they become properly involved their hands will "just naturally" do the correct things. This diagnosis is amusing. It amounts to saying that once things get better, things will get better. For anyone other than professional actors or highly experienced amateurs, these types of analyses are not much help. Yet, few of us are content to wait and hope. We want to know how we can *help* solve the problem.

The most common solutions to the problem of awkward hands are not necessarily the best. The classic approach is to give actors something to do: fiddling with a cane, washing dishes, sweeping the floor, playing with a handkerchief, crossing their arms, putting their hands on their hips, and so on. No matter how ingenious they may be, unless such actions are

One way for actors to experiment with proper and effective use of the hands is the "Come here!" exercise.

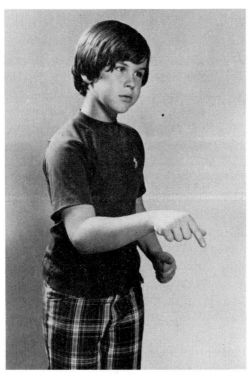

By creating a series of different hand and arm gestures for the simple, two-word line "Come here!," actors can develop greater sensitivity to the problems of gesture and hand movement.

carefully created and judiciously used, there will be a tendency for this kind of theatrical business to degenerate into meaningless "busy-ness." Nor does it help to encourage erring actors to simply forget about their hands. More often than not, this will completely confound already self-conscious actors whose basic problem is they *can't* forget about their hands. Finally, don't assume that any difficulty will somehow work itself out before opening night. Chance and the muses are notoriously unreliable at last minute rescues.

The best solution is to demonstrate that proper and effective use of the hands is vital to the creation of a role and can be an important factor in communicating the meaning of many lines. It's necessary to realize that inexperienced performers often need to be told this. An excellent way to get these points across is to involve the actor in something called the "Come here!" exercise. By creating or performing a series of different hand and arm gestures for the simple, two-word line "Come here!", actors can develop their sensitivity to the problems of gesture and hand movement. They can also learn to develop their roles by imagining and rehearsing how their characters might gesture if they were to say "Come here!" to various other characters in the play in specific situations.

What sort of gestures? On the word "come," a student can extend his right arm straight out from the front of his body with his index finger pointing at the face of the person being addressed. On the word "here," the wrist is flipped downward at a ninety degree angle so that the index finger is pointing at the floor. Or, he can hold his hand six or eight inches in front of his chest and wiggle his index finger in a "come hither" fashion. Finally, he can create another more urgent feeling by curving his right arm around in front of his body, palm inward, and rapidly waving his arm from his elbow parallel to the floor.

You can undoubtedly come up with other phrases and gestures. Give as many as you think will be useful, emphasizing the fact that the manner in which the actor gestures will almost always strongly affect the sense of the line. In fact, some gestures will literally force actors to change their line readings.

This rather simple exercise, if properly handled, helps an actor appreciate the importance of gesture. But it is necessary to remember that it is only an initial step. Under no circumstances give young actors the impression that they will be required to pantomime the meaning of every line. This will justifiably increase their confusion. Instead, they should be encouraged to use gestures that will help them create and express their roles. In other words, the focus of gestures is not necessarily on what any particular line means but on who is saying it.

A helpful technique at this point is to teach the actors to *zone* their hands and arms—to move them only within certain prescribed limits. If

Students can learn to develop their roles by experimenting with how their characters would say "Come here!" in different circumstances.

The manner in which the actor gestures will almost always strongly affect the sense of the line.

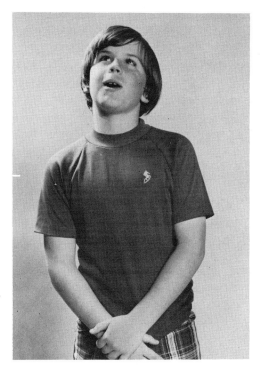

Under no circumstances should you give young actors the impression that they must pantomime the meaning of every line.

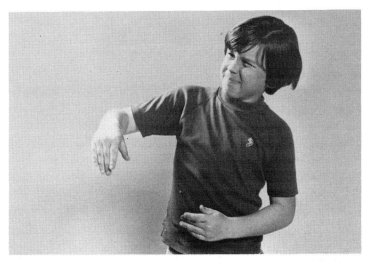

Students should be encouraged to use gestures that will help them create and express their ideas.

The focus of any gesture is not necessarily on what any particular line means but on who is saying it.

The hands of some students droop lifelessly at their sides.

A helpful technique is to teach the actors to zone their hands and arms—to move them only within certain prescribed limits.

these zones are carefully chosen and cleverly presented, actors may discover that their hands are not awkward liabilities, but significant tools that can be used to help discover and create characters.

For example, a zone can be created by telling an actress to hold her hands out from her body with her elbows bent and her palms or wrists facing upwards. While gesturing, her hands may be turned over or moved in front of her body. The hands should not be moved below the waist or above the shoulders. After some practice, the actress using this zone may begin to feel more elegant or regal.

It is essential to recognize that these zones do not have specific "meanings." The actor is not taught to gesture in one prescribed way to portray elegance, or in another to portray sadness, and so on. The interpretations of each zone given here are intended only as examples of how an actor might use them. More importantly, zoning is a general technique for teaching and encouraging actors to create their characters by using gesture.

Another useful zone can be created if the performer holds his upper

This student experiments with a zone extending from his waist to his chest. In addition, he tries to keep his hands and arms out to the left and right of his body.

When asked to face his palms down, he begins to discover some new dimensions.

Asked to face palms up, he discovers even more.

Hands held at shoulder height, with the palms up, is not this student's usual way of gesturing, but as an actor, he finds it useful.

With a little practice, you can help performers create zones that are suited to their specific characterizations and acting abilities.

Zoning is most useful for actors who are self-conscious about their hands and gestures. It is a technique designed to turn this kind of misplaced concentration into a method for improving performance.

arms close to the sides of his body and keeps his forearms more or less perpendicular to the floor, with his palms facing his body. Using this zone, actors may begin to feel more "Mediterranean." This work can help actors establish fiery Spanish or Italian characters.

This last zone can be given a completely different feeling if the actor simply turns his palms so that they are facing away from his body. In effect, a new zone is created. The resulting gestures are likely to suit a talkative, emphatic or preachy character. In fact, turning the wrists one hundred and eighty degrees is an extremely useful way in which to alter any zone.

Zoning can also be used to help performers who tend to overact. By creating small zones (a two foot square in front of the chest or not allowing the actor's hands to go above waist level), overactors can usually be "toned down." As actors demonstrate more control of their roles, they can be encouraged to break away, little by little, from complete reliance on zoning. This uncomplicated technique is almost always surprisingly effective.

With a little practice, you can help performers create zones that are suited to their specific characterizations and acting abilities. It is important to note that these zones are not static poses in the manner of the old "point" books or pseudo-scientifically organized units of expression of the infamous Delsarte system.

Zoning is most useful for actors who are self-conscious about their hands and gestures. It is a technique designed to turn this kind of misplaced concentration into a method for improving performance. If you are willing to utilize it, you may be in a better position to help the next performer who interrupts a rehearsal scene, squints out into the auditorium to find you and asks ". . .but what do I do with my hands?"

Some Further Thoughts

Even those uninhibited students who feel perfectly free to create their characters often don't know how to go about doing it. Acting students need specific techniques that will help them to stimulate and control their imaginative processes. The goal of the exercises in this chapter is to get student/actors on their feet and working on their characters rather than simply talking about working on their characters.

Sometimes, one of these techniques will work with a particular student while another will fail to make the slightest impression. Sometimes all three techniques will fail abysmally. No technique is infallible and directors need to learn as many methods as possible for stimulating the imaginations of their students. Although the directorial qualities of enthusiasm and sincerity are helpful to students tackling the problems of playing their first roles, they are not enough to replace directorial knowledge and skill.

6

Character Analysis: A Short Course in the Stanislavsky System

Directors usually bring to the task of analyzing a play for production knowledge of a wide variety of methods and techniques that can help to make their job a little easier. After noting the general type of play (e.g., comedy, tragedy, melodrama, etc.) as well as the time period and locations in which it is set, perhaps the most important thing for a director to have is a clear awareness of the play's plot. Most simply, the plot of any play can be thought of as *who does what to whom in what order?* It is always the director's responsibility to make certain that this information is clearly conveyed to the audience.

When working with seven to eleven year old actors and audience members, a clear presentation and appreciation of the plot of a play is often all that can reasonably be expected. Beyond this level, however, questions concerning the why of the action—that is, the *motivations* of the characters—become increasingly important to the performers as well as to their audiences. At this point, it is part of the director/teacher's job to help the performers understand and express such motivations in ways that can be seen, heard, and appreciated by the audience.

The most famous system of helping actors to understand and communicate the motivations of their characters was developed by the great

Russian actor, acting teacher and director, Constantine Stanislavsky (1863-1938). The Stanislavsky system is only one technique among many that can be adapted by director/teachers to help young performers understand more about motivating their characters.

The elements of Stanislavsky's system that are explained in this chapter can be introduced to junior high school students who have already had considerable theatrical experience. The concepts are difficult, but director/teachers who want to help their more advanced student actors will need some understanding of them.

Stanislavsky's use of the terms *super-objective, objective, unit* and *beat,* is an aspect of his system that can be particularly helpful when working with older students. His system is based on the assumption that stage characters must be much more consistent than real people if they are to sustain the interest of an audience.

To help achieve this quality, Stanislavsky taught his actors the importance of finding or creating a single, overall goal or *super-objective* for every character in every play. Always briefly and clearly phrased in terms of a concrete, active question (e.g., "How can I become king?"), the super-objective must be a consistent and unambiguous reference point for the *entire* role.

For example, is Hamlet's super-objective "How can I avenge my father's death?", "How can I save Denmark from corruption and tyranny?", or "How can I become king in my uncle's place?" (*Hamlet* is used as an example only because it is difficult to think of a children's play that is likely to be so universally recognized.) No one statement of Hamlet's—or any character's—super-objective is the one and only correct one, but only one can be chosen. The super-objective that is chosen will be the single most important factor in determining a character's moods, style, relationships and motivations. This is where the art of interpretation begins.

The super-objective must be further divided into a number of smaller parts call *objectives*. An objective is a character's reason for being in a specific scene or group of scenes. In the theater, no character comes or stays on stage without a reason. In cooperation with the director, the actor determines a step by step plan of action; each step must conform to the super-objective.

Objectives are an important part of an actor's creation and must be chosen with care to their: (1) rightness for the play and the character, (2) the degree to which they provide emotional stimulation for the actor, and (3) how well they will appeal to an audience. Perhaps Hamlet's first objective would be to investigate the role that his uncle, Claudius, played in his father's death. There are innumerable ways to phrase Hamlet's objective at this point. The actor's final choice (again, always done in concert with the director) will help him to create, understand, and make plausible the character's actions.

Does Hamlet want to prove Claudius innocent? Does he want to prove Claudius guilty? Does he genuinely want to discover if Claudius is innocent or guilty? If the actor playing Hamlet wants to find Claudius innocent, then the audience will, perhaps, be more inclined to see Hamlet as a procrastinator. If Hamlet is predisposed to find his uncle guilty, then perhaps he will be perceived as more ambitious and decisive. If it is decided that Hamlet really wants to be certain as to Claudius' guilt or innocence then the audience will most likely think of him as a genuine seeker of truth, a self-sacrificing crusader for his country, and an ideal of justice.

Clearly, some of these objectives are more appropriate to one of our super-objectives than to the others. For example, the Hamlet whose objective is to find his uncle guilty will likely have as his super-objective the desire to become king. On the other hand, the Hamlet whose objective is to determine his uncle's guilt or innocence is more likely to have as his super-objective the desire to save Denmark from tyranny and corruption. It should also be easy to understand how the choice of a particular super-objective will make the choice of certain objectives seem unlikely, implausible or inconsistent, and will tend to confuse the actors and the audience.

Any objective of any character must be further divided into *units*. A unit stands in much the same relationship to an objective that an objective does to a super-objective. A unit is also of much the same quality as an objective, but of shorter duration. While an objective might apply to an entire scene, a unit might apply for only a paragraph or sentence. There is no precise formula for determining the duration of any of Stanislavsky's elements. A great deal must be left to the judgment of the actor and director.

For example, after seeing and speaking with his father's ghost, Hamlet tells certain friendly members of the palace guard that he is going to "put an antic disposition on"—in other words, that he is going to feign madness. But what is his motivation for this statement? Is he slyly trying to conceal the fact that the ghost's startling revelations have in fact driven him insane? Is he operating on the principle that if he is thought mad, he will more easily get away with the murder of his uncle? Is he planning to investigate his uncle while hiding behind a protective shield of "madness?" Is he going to try to draw his uncle out into the open by saying and doing a number of things that only a madman would be permitted to say and do? The eventual choice of any one of these units must be considered and structured in relation to a set of previously chosen objectives and a super-objective.

The smallest definable motivational link in the chain that Stanislavsky built is called a *beat*. For example, Hamlet has just driven his sword through the draperies in his mother's room to stab a man he believes is Claudius. He draws the cloth aside only to discover that the victim is not Claudius but his former sweetheart's father, Polonius. Is he sad, happy, or unconcerned over his error? Once more, no one answer is necessarily right or wrong. But one answer must be chosen, and the decision cannot help but effect the actor's interpretation and the audience's appreciation and understanding of a very important moment in the play. The character's motivation at this instant must also be clear, intelligent and plausible in the light of everything else that he has said and done so far.

After determining the super-objective and possibly a few of the more significant objectives, the actor moves toward a consistent and complete awareness of the role in terms of units and beats, by utilizing what Stanislavsky called the *magic if*. Use of the magic if requires actors who are having difficulty developing a particular scene or moment to ask themselves the following question: "If *I* were the character in this situation, how would I feel and what would I do?" As the actor rehearses the play, he or she continually keeps this question in mind. By this means, the magic if serves to help inspire, organize, and discipline the actor's creation of a role. More importantly, the magic if helps the actor keep a handle on the character in warmly human rather than coldly intellectual terms.

For example, Hamlet has been joking with some very funny grave-makers. In the process of digging a fresh grave, they have had to disturb some old bones. They are all having a fine time. A gravedigger throws out an old skull. Hamlet picks it up and out of idle, good humored curiosity, asks whose skull it was. It turns out to have belonged to Yorick, court jester to Hamlet's father and, more importantly, Hamlet's favorite child-hood playmate. The actor playing Hamlet must now ask: "If I were Hamlet, and I unexpectedly discovered that I was holding the skull of an old friend in my hands, how would *I* feel and what would *I* do?"

Good actors know how easy it is to *say* lines without understanding their emotional content. The magic if, in combination with super-objectives, objectives, units and beats, is the substance of an extremely effective system for dealing with this problem.

Although for purposes of convenience we have used *Hamlet* as our example, it should be easy to see how these elements of Stanislavsky's system could be used to help an older student create a complicated but dramatically consistent character in any play. Like all techniques, this system gives a performer greater control over his or her art. There is always an element of instinct in any artist. But the best artists must learn how to temper and develop their instincts with knowledge, technique, and hard work. As Stanislavsky himself admitted, the best techniques act as spurs to inspiration and emotional commitment, not as substitutes for them.

7

Developing Concentration

Through concentration, trained actors can make their emotions and their bodies more responsive to their wills. The introductory exercises in Chapters Two and Five simply demonstrated that actors must pay attention to what they are doing—a fact that is not always clear to those who believe that actors need only do what comes naturally. The exercises in this chapter are intended for use with older and more advanced students and serve two additional purposes. First, they can give actors an internal awareness of the fact that stage concentration is an intense and exhilarating process. Actors can then use this awareness as a reference point for judging the effectiveness of their own stage concentration at any particular moment. Second, the exercises can help actors *commit* themselves to their roles and stage emotions.

The technique I use is strongly based on the research findings of Theodore X. Barber of the Medfield Foundation in Medfield, Massachusetts. Dr. Barber, a psychologist, has shown that most people respond extremely well to suggestions that elicit their cooperation, motivate them, give them positive attitudes about the situation and lead them to think that they will be able to perform the suggested tasks. Keeping these factors in mind can be of great value in helping student actors respond to a particular suggestion or achieve a specific effect.

Before beginning the exercises, I explain how they fit into a concept of the "total actor." As mentioned in Chapter Five, it is impossible to summarize all of the techniques and methods actors can use to build a character, but the art of acting has two major aspects: the internal and external.

With the external aspect, actors begin by trying to create the outward form of their characters. They must design their make-up and study their costumes. They concentrate on developing a walk, hand gestures and habitual facial movements. They may borrow a hand gesture from one person and a particular style of walking from another, or they may create everything from their own imaginations. No movement, gesture or physical quirk can be unnecessary. Every external nuance must be derived from a clear concept of the character and must serve a dramatic function. When some kind of external composite is completed, the actor tries to discover clues about how the character thinks and feels based on how he or she looks and moves.

For example, the male actor in a Restoration comedy learns many gestures and details of elegant seventeenth century behavior: the way to bow, the way to take snuff, the way to hold a walking stick. The actor's task is not simply to perform these skills but to use them in molding his characterization. These mechanically learned gestures and postures can provide him with subtle insights into his role.

The internal aspect begins with the actors' abilities to imagine themselves into their roles. They may think: "If I were really this character in this situation, then this is the way I would think and behave." Or, they may base their interpretations on their own experiences in similar situations. For example, in order to play someone who has lost his or her way in the forest, an actor may vividly recall an actual situation in the past when he or she was really lost in the woods.

Actors must be trained to respond to their own suggestions and those of their directors in order to create and control their characterizations. In turn, gesture and movement will often emerge more clearly as an actor's thoughts and feelings find expression.

Very few acting techniques are exclusively derived from either the external or the internal aspect. For example, the Stanislavsky system as outlined in Chapter Six clearly involves both. Whatever their training, most actors feel that various combinations of the two aspects must be used.

No matter how an actor approaches his or her character, a key element is always concentration—the disciplined and intense commitment to discovering and portraying all aspects of that character.

Once the students have learned the theory behind the concentration exercises, they are ready for what Dr. Barber has called "task motivational instructions." These task motivational instructions help actors to understand how it feels to really concentrate.

I normally assemble the acting class or cast and lead them through the

While the teacher gives instructions, a student concentrates on making her arm as rigid as a bar or iron or a steel girder.

motivational exercises myself. The students should stand up straight with feet at shoulder width, eyes closed and right arms raised over their heads. Then, I give more specific instructions in a gentle but firm tone: "Clench your fist. Tightly. As you clench your fist, you will discover that your arm is becoming more and more rigid like a bar of iron or a steel girder. Try to bend your arm." Some will bend their arms and others won't. To those who haven't bent their arms, I say "Try harder." Some will apparently be trying very hard to bend their arms—without success. "All right, now you can bend your arm. Sure, it's easy. Of course you can bend your arm. All right, now let's discuss what happened."

The ensuing, often animated discussion, reveals the presence of three different groups: those for whom the exercise did not work at all; those who were sure that they could have bent their arms but didn't; and those who felt that they really couldn't bend their arms. A little probing normally shows that those in the last group were thinking along the following lines: "My arm is very rigid like an iron bar or a steel girder. It is very, very rigid. My arm is a steel girder. I can't bend it. Wait a second, my arm is an arm. I can so bend it."

Those who didn't respond may say that they knew it wasn't going to work for them and they weren't surprised when they didn't respond to the suggestions. At this point, I stress that it is very easy to fight the suggestions. The idea is to want to go along, to try to go along. This kind of explanation is often helpful to those who initially found it difficult to respond. Concentration is more than the process of creating or listening to imaginative suggestions. It requires intense *commitment* to those suggestions.

Do a few more exercises: "Your eyelids are getting heavier and heavier. Heavier and heavier. They are falling shut. They are very heavy. So heavy that it seems as though they are stuck or glued together. Glued or stuck together so tightly that if I asked you to try and open them you wouldn't be able to. In a moment, I'm going to ask you to open your eyes and you won't be able to. Go ahead, try to open your eyes." Some actors will open their eyes, others will keep them closed without appearing to try to open them, and yet others will not be able to open them despite a great deal of apparent strain. At this point, I say: "All right now, you can open your eyes. Come on, just open your eyes."

These particular exercises always intrigue acting students. They now know how it feels to concentrate. They have experienced the importance of cooperation with the director and of positive motivation and positive attitudes within an exercise situation. Follow these first exercises with a discussion of some of the problems involved in developing concentration. You may want to consider some of the following points.

The most common type of misplaced concentration which most actors can understand occurs when students prepare to take an examination. Often, they will find themselves concentrating on concentrating rather than concentrating on the material to be learned: "I need an A on this exam." or "If I don't get at least a B on the test, I'm going to flunk the course." Although we could probably agree that such thoughts are directly related to the examination, it's easy to see how they could interfere with the processes of studying for it.

A similar tendency to misplace or misuse concentration is common among student actors. If there is a particular moment at which an actor is supposed to cry, he or she may be thinking: "I've got to cry now. If I don't, this scene is going to fall flat and the whole point of the act may be lost." What actors should do, of course, is involve their characters in the moment, concentrating on the sadness of it until it genuinely affects them.

After this kind of discussion, move on to an image or role exercise. These are slightly more complicated than the exercises already discussed. They provide a transition between relatively simple classroom concentration games and genuinely complex problems of concentrating on stage: "Close your eyes and relax. As you relax, you can feel yourself getting younger and younger. Younger and younger until you are four years old. You are four years old and sitting in this room listening to me. And you're bored. So bored." Most of the students will quickly assume the character of a bored four year old. "O.K. Now you're getting older and older and you're back to your own age again. Let's talk about what we're doing some more."

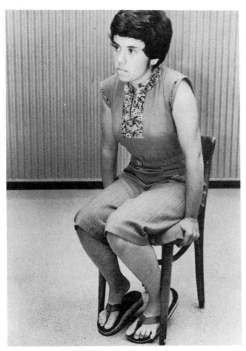

The student concentrates on being stuck to the chair so that she cannot stand up.

The actors may now ask: "This is all fine if we are listening to you, but how can we do it ourselves?" The answer is simple: "You heard the suggestions that I gave to you and remember them. Just give one of the suggestions to yourselves. Go ahead, try it." Spend a few minutes while everyone experiments with simple suggestions such as "I cannot bend my arm." or "I cannot get up from my chair."

Now the students are ready for specific *emotion* exercises. Because these are more difficult, some sort of transition or buffer suggestion is often necessary. For example, first suggest that the actors are four year old or ninety-four years old and *then* add a further suggestion that they are happy or sad: "Something is very funny here. It's really very funny. It's so funny that soon you are going to laugh. In fact, you're beginning to laugh now. Go on, laugh out loud." A surprising number of people will begin to laugh quite easily and naturally. At this point, you can tell them to stop laughing. Or you can lead them in another direction: "Wait a minute. This is not funny at all. It's terrible. Terrible and sad. You've made an awful mistake and it makes you feel so ashamed. It's so sad, so very sad that you want to cry. You can feel yourself not wanting to cry but you know that you will." You can improvise further. Crying usually takes longer than laughing, but if you give it enough time, a good number of people will respond. Work back and forth between suggestions to cry and suggestions to laugh until it takes only a few moments for actors to respond to either suggestion. The students are invariably surprised at the speed and ease with which they can make this seemingly difficult emotional transition. With a little practice, many will quickly learn to perform these actions alone.

Occasionally, some actors will get so involved in the exercises that it will be necessary to repeat the instructions to break concentration several times. If the actor is working on a difficult moment repeat the instructions to break concentration in a calm voice until the actor complies: "There's nothing there at all. You can open your eyes and look at me. You feel just fine." Work until actors can give themselves suggestions. You can even create original suggestions suited to a specific role or the acting problems of a particular actor. Using the methods explained here, I have had success teaching actors how to do such things as laugh and cry on stage—convincingly and on cue.

There is nothing mysterious about why this technique works so well. Most people, when they are positively motivated will respond extraordinarily well to direct suggestions. By using these concentration exercises, student actors learn to discipline and control their thought processes, skills, and imaginations during all phases of rehearsal and performance.

8

Acting and Hand Puppetry

There is more to hand puppetry than making a few puppets and moving them around in semi-improvised theaters made from scraps of fabric and painted refrigerator cartons. Yet few books or articles on the subject attempt to develop more than a basic awareness of hand puppetry techniques. Many authors seem to assume that a puppet production is so easy to mount that any advice on the subject is more or less unnecessary. But so many performers—amateurs and professionals alike—never seem to conquer the basic problems.

Perhaps the most important thing to remember is that puppeteers are actors. They retain the responsibilities of examining text and subtext, of creating viable and stageworthy characters and, naturally, of learning their lines. Nonetheless, many "professional" puppeteers do none of these things. Blocking is not planned, lines are not memorized and other than being "cute," the puppets have no characters. Aspiring actors as well as puppeteers must understand that puppetry is a difficult and precise theater art.

The Value of Puppetry to Actors

Those of us who teach acting are well aware that the transition from exercises that lead toward public performance to the actual performance

Performing with puppets allows students to create and express characters, relationships and situations without the gnawing feeling that they are being prematurely exposed to public criticism.

itself is a crucial stage. It is at this point that the student actor is most likely to "freeze" or feel inhibited. Performance with hand puppets is a useful method for helping actors through this important phase. It provides a trial arena that tends to increase an actor's confidence and effectiveness under performance conditions.

Puppet theater performance allows students to create and express characters, relationships and situations without the gnawing feeling that they are being prematurely exposed to public criticism. Since the actors are hidden from the sight of the audience, they can feel slightly less pressured and can concentrate more easily on developing the characters and the situations in accordance with the play that they have chosen.

The point is to place students in a situation in which they feel highly motivated to create, rather than forcing them into a situation which intimidates them or makes them feel unprepared. The first situation builds confidence while the second often fosters the kinds of inhibitions and restraints that the students may never fully overcome.

This chapter is a brief discussion of puppet characterization, scripting, rehearsal procedures, script analysis, and manipulation. The kind of puppet theater performance described assumes some knowledge of basic acting techniques on the part of the teacher and the students. Its goals are limited to helping actors cope with the presence of an audience. Because of this, many problems of full-scale puppet theater production—scenic and costume design, lighting, etc.—are not covered. For the purposes of this chapter at least, such considerations are beside the point.

Where can you get good script material? What qualities should it have?

Provided it has speaking roles, action and audience appeal, any story, play or poem that appeals to your students can become material for a puppet production. A particularly good example of a poem that has all the necessary qualities is Lewis Carroll's "The Walrus and the Carpenter."

In this case, the roles are obvious: the Walrus, the Carpenter, some oysters, and a narrator. The narrator, who can be either a puppet or a student standing in front of the theater, speaks all the lines, including the "he saids" and "they saids" that are not specifically assigned to one of the characters in the poem.

I have always chosen poems, stories or plays that can be acted by no less than three but no more than six students. If there are too few roles, the exercise degenerates into a static and uninteresting monologue; if there are too many, it will become a chaotic muddle.

The actions in "The Walrus and the Carpenter" are as clearly defined as the roles themselves. The characters walk, talk, eat and cry. Students

A particularly good example of a poem that has all the necessary qualities to make a puppet play is Lewis Carroll's "The Walrus and the Carpenter." *Photo by David L. Young.*

need action as a reference point for their interpretations and performances. They will probably spend a great deal of rehearsal time discussing what each character *does*. During the first stages of the activity, the interpretation of what each character can do is what the students will find most interesting.

"The Walrus and the Carpenter" is ideal for the middle grades—four, five, and six. The younger the students, the simpler and more clearly defined the action should be. Older students, on the other hand, are likely to become bored unless you offer them some rather complicated and subtle dramatic action either in terms of more sophisticated direction or more "adult" material. Combined song and story versions of folk tales like "John Henry" or "Barbara Allen" are particularly useful.

How to Handle the Technical Problems

After a suitable script has been prepared, it is time to make or acquire the puppets. Hand puppets are the easiest to make and use.

Although many teachers would probably prefer that the students make their own puppets, I always make them myself. Making puppets in the classroom too often switches the focus from actor training to the craft of puppet making.

A recent publication that provides valuable information on making hand puppets is *Making Glove Puppets* by Esme McLaren (Plays, Inc., Boston). You will find that papier mâché, fabric scraps, acrylic paints,

To make a very simple puppet theater, use a utility knife to cut away the top, bottom and one side of a refrigerator or stove carton.

A simple cardboard stage can be easily painted in just a few minutes.

brushes and a little effort are all that you need to create genuinely beautiful puppets.

Although children are fascinated by even the simplest puppets, I have found that the more appealing and professional-looking they are, the more students want to use them. It's a good idea to avoid standard characters or popular styles. Original puppets encourage the students to think of each puppet script as something unique and individual, while the use of familiar, commercial Walt Disney or Muppet characters encourages easy imitation.

The construction of a suitable hand puppet theater is no problem at all. Any store that sells large appliances will probably be glad to donate a refrigerator or stove carton that can be cut down to size, painted and made into a surprisingly durable "theater" in just a few minutes' time. Use a utility knife to cut away the top, bottom and one side of the box. During performance, students will hold the puppets above the upper edge of a simple, three-sided booth. Use of the three or four foot long top of the box provides space for a number of people to work comfortably. The common practice of cutting a television-screen-sized hole in front of the box

95

This imaginative teacher designed two simple yet permanent hand puppet theaters that can be stored and reused.

This extremely simple hand puppet stage can be clamped to a table.

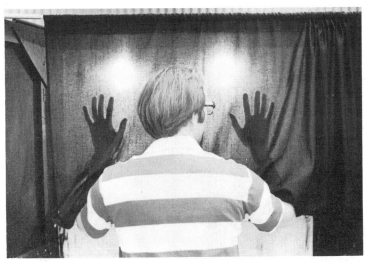

The puppeteer stands behind a piece of black cloth. With the light coming from the front of the stage, the puppeteer can easily see the puppets but the audience cannot see the puppeteer.

stifles effective movement of the puppets. In addition, having three to six students trying to move around the tiny stage opening creates enormous difficulties.

A great many common rehearsal and performance problems can be circumvented in advance by the design of the backstage area of the puppet theater. Yet all too often this vital aspect of performance is given little or no serious consideration. It's a good idea to reserve special attention for three factors in the design of any puppet theater. They are *order, quiet,* and *convenience.*

The need for *order* is paramount. Everything backstage must have its own special place. The puppeteers should be able to get at anything they may need without having to move something else in order to get it. During performance, when they are concentrating on acting and on moving the play along smoothly, there won't be time for them to dive into a pile of puppets to find the hero, or to grope through a disorganized pile of properties for the right object. Once a puppet or a property has been used during a performance, it should be put back in its own special place.

This kind of order makes it much easier to maintain *quiet* backstage. There will be no heaps of puppets and props that can clatter easily to the floor where they'll get lost in the darkness and prompt a noisy, panic-stricken search.

Convenience is the factor that can make the difference between a good show and an excellent show. How fast can the puppeteers put one puppet

In a professional hand puppet theater, the need for order is paramount. The puppeteer should be able to get at anything he needs without moving something else in order to get it.

down and pick another up? How quickly and easily can they operate the light board? Are there situations when it is too easy to hit the wrong switch or pick up the wrong puppet? A convenient design is one that minimizes the possibilities for errors, and eliminates unnecessary work during performance.

Those interested in more advanced techniques will be interested in the following suggestions. They are meant to be applied to the use of some of the more permanent theaters shown in the accompanying photographs. Sew a large curtain ring into the rear hem of each puppet. Even with one hand, it is easy to slide these rings on and off bathroom hooks strategically hung backstage. Heavy fabric hung between the front wall of the theater and the puppets eliminates the bumping and scraping noises that could occur during performance if the solid heads of the puppets were allowed to come into contact with the walls of the theater.

Properties can be placed in order on a low shelf on the right side of the theater. Incidentally, this "shelf" can be the suitcase into which the puppets or properties are packed when the curtain is down.

Placing a small light board to the puppeteers' right on a level just below the playing area lets them perform light cues easily. Puppet theaters should be designed specifically for the person or group that will be using them. A little forethought in designing the theater can help to minimize and avoid many problems in staging and manipulation.

How are Rehearsals Handled?

When my students arrive one morning, they find a number of simple hand puppet theaters set up in various places around the room. On a table or desk in front of each theater are mimeographed copies of a specific poem, story, play, or other script material. Along with each set of scripts or script materials is a corresponding set of puppets. Since I now have enough puppets for an entire class, I no longer plan alternate activities for my students. Formerly, I provided multiple activities from which the students could choose, explaining that everyone would eventually have a chance to join in the puppet activity.

Next, I divide the class into "production units" and suggest that they read their scripts and examine their puppets for a few minutes. After five or ten minutes, I visit each production unit individually. By the time I get to them, many of the groups have already discussed the scripts and assigned roles.

If the preparation time has been well spent, students as young as nine years old can be left pretty much to themselves to handle many rehearsal problems. They should feel free, however, to seek guidance from the teacher.

During preliminary rehearsals, there should be considerable discussion concerning basic production points. With primary graders, this usually consists of what actions are performed, who performs them and who says what lines.

Older students who may be handling more complicated scripts will have more challenging problems. Of course, it's important to discuss the basic points, but there are other considerations. For example: What actions are performed in the poem, story or play? Which are only described? In "The Walrus and the Carpenter," for example, the characters actually go for a walk and eat, but they only describe what the "seven maids with seven mops" do. There are other potentially interesting issues: Where does the action take place? What kinds of personalities do the chief characters have? Are they calm? What are the relationships between the characters? Do they like one another? Are they arguing? What *voices* do the puppets use? Assigning a voice to each puppet character is a special problem. Many performers instinctively reach for ostensibly cute "puppet" voices by creating unnaturally high-pitched, very low-pitched, or strangely husky voices. Although these solutions to the problem of speaking shouldn't be ruled out, a puppet's voice will be most effective when it is derived from a concept of its character. Dialects, vocal patterns and speech rhythms can also be used to great advantage. An audience is likely to find even the prettiest of puppets with the "cutest" of voices boring unless these traits are part of a vital, integrated characterization.

Blocking and Manipulation

After the characters and their motivations have been analyzed, the students rehearse the puppets' blocking and manipulation. Blocking a puppet play requires the same care and attention as blocking a play with live actors. (See Chapter Four.)

Generally speaking, it is good practice to block some movement for the puppet that is talking while keeping puppets that are not talking as still as possible. The old stage adage, "Don't move on another actor's line," remains particularly valid in the puppet theater. With two or more puppets bobbing around it is difficult for even the most attentive member of the audience to figure out which one is supposed to be speaking. All of the characters' actions and emotions must be expressed clearly and imaginatively. One way to check clarity is to perform the script without words. If the essential actions are not understandable, some reworking may be necessary. Intense discussions often result from this, as the students weigh one movement pattern against another.

After blocking patterns have been determined, the students should rehearse the manipulation of their puppets with great care. Manipulation is easier when students know a few "tricks of the trade."

For example, although it is possible to work hand puppets while sitting or kneeling, most knowledgeable performers prefer to work standing up. The more mobile the puppeteer, the more easily he or she can move the puppets. A simple illustration should clarify this point. If a sitting puppeteer wants the puppet on his right hand to move left and the puppet on his left hand to move right, he must cross his arms in an extremely awkward manner. The standing puppeteer can perform the same action with greater ease and grace by simply turning around and facing the back of the theater.

Another point that many beginners overlook is that hand puppeteers often have to keep their arms extended over their heads for substantial periods of time. Weak-armed puppeteers will lower a puppet little by

The author demonstrates that it is possible for the puppeteer to work while sitting down . . . .

But getting the "actors" to change sides of the stage becomes an awkward proposition.

The standing puppeteer can accomplish the same cross much more easily and gracefully . . .

little until only its head can be seen by the audience. Until students develop a puppeteer's strength they will have to resist the very strong temptation to prop the puppet into position by resting their arms against the lower edge of the stage. Obviously they cannot rest their arms and manipulate the puppets effectively at the same time. On the other hand, if they do get the chance to relax their arms for a moment—and they can do it without interrupting the flow of the performance—they should by all means relax. They will probably welcome it, and when their arms are rested they will be able to manipulate their puppets much more easily and expressively.

With a little training, fourth graders and older students can develop the strength necessary to hold their arms above their heads for a half to three quarters of an hour at a time. This feat is not as difficult as it may sound if the performer is willing to rehearse for about forty-five minutes a day for two weeks before the first performance.

Once the student puppeteers develop the necessary strength they must learn the significance of the terms *straight, firm,* and *steady. Straight* refers to the puppeteer's ability to hold his or her figure vertical in relation

... by simply rotating his body 180 degrees (back to the audience), and swiveling his hands a half-turn to the front.

to the stage floor. Neither the puppet's head nor its body should be tilted to the left or right, or foreward or backward unless such a movement or posture is needed. *Firm* refers to control. There should be no unintentional shaking, wilting, or drooping of the figure. Purposeful movement is a vital factor in the creation of mood and meaning. All too often figures are moved senselessly and aimlessly about the stage as though any movement were dramatically significant. Good puppeteers realize the importance of being especially careful in this area. The puppeteer need only wiggle his or her fingers to make the puppet move its arms. This means that tiny movements on the part of the puppeteer may take on a greatly amplified significance when they are considered in relation to the puppet. Even very small movements can, if they are not carefully planned, often read as sloppiness or carelessness.

Steady refers to the puppet's stage position. It is most important that audiences see neither more nor less of the puppet than the puppeteer wants them to see. This means that the figures must be held neither too high nor too low with reference to sight lines. Each figure must also be held in a proper and sensible relationship to the other puppets so that no

The puppeteer's wrist joint gives the puppets their most expressive and expansive movements.

one of them appears too tall or too short. The audience will lose interest quickly if all they can see is the top of a puppet's head. Nor are they particularly interested in looking at the puppeteer's forearm or elbow sticking out beneath the puppet's costume. Finally, a good student puppeteer should be able to hold a puppet still for as long as three or four minutes—even though he or she may be actively manipulating a second puppet with his or her other hand.

Once these general principles have been mastered, there are a number of technical tricks that may help student puppeteers solve specific staging problems. For example, when using puppets with solid heads (made from wood, papier mâché, Sculptamold or other hard materials), the puppet's head can be turned independently of its body when the inside rim of its neck is squeezed between the puppeteer's thumb and forefinger. If the thumb is squeezed towards the tip of the index finger, the head will turn in one direction. If the thumb is squeezed towards the base of the index finger, the head will turn in the opposite direction. Naturally, this technique will work only if the head is light enough to move easily, the neck hole is fitted to the operator's fingers, and the fabric around the base of the puppet's neck is not so stiff or thick that it will impede movement.

It is also important for student puppeteers to practice wrist movement. The wrist joint gives the puppets their most expressive and expansive movements. Slight turns of the wrist can create a great variety of expression—even with a solid faced puppet. The emotional significance of any particular hand movement can vary widely, depending on the puppet being used.

Above all, do not forget that the manipulation of hand puppets is an art in itself. An ancient saying among Chinese hand puppeteers is: "There are many professions in the world, but the hardest to master is the art of *Pu-tai-hsi* (hand puppetry)." Nonetheless, it is necessary to begin somewhere. A useful source for further information on hand puppet manipulation is *Making Hand Puppets Come Alive: A Method of Learning and Teaching Hand Puppets*, authored by Carol Fijan and Larry Engler.

Performance

The amount of rehearsal time for this puppet unit will vary con-

Slight turns of the wrist can create a great variety of expression—even with a solid-faced puppet.

Students practice different ways to hold their hands when using puppets.

siderably. Nine-year-olds can rarely make effective use of more than an hour or two of minimally supervised rehearsal. On the other hand, highly motivated fourteen year olds who expect a polished performance may demand twelve to fourteen hours of rehearsal time. Only the individual teacher is qualified to gauge what would be most appropriate.

In any event, at a prearranged day and time, each production unit performs its play for the rest of the class. After everyone has performed, fifteen to twenty minutes should be spent in constructive criticism, such as: "If the actor who played the dragon in the second play had held his puppet higher, it would have been easier to see." "If the actor playing Jennifer in the first play had spoken a little more slowly, she would have been easier to understand," and so forth. The older the students and the more time and effort they spend on rehearsals, the more probing the criticism can and should be.

Conclusion

As with other lessons in this book, it is important for teachers and

106

students to understand that the puppetry unit is one step towards a larger process, not a goal in itself.

Puppetry and acting are related but separate arts. This chapter has not explained a method for training puppeteers. Instead, it outlines a simple style of hand puppetry that can be used to help train actors. If along the way a student or two develops an enthusiasm for puppet theater, no one will complain.

9

Readers Theater: An Alternative Stage

A readers theater production that combines simple oral interpretation, basic acting techniques, and imaginative staging can be much easier to manage, yet just as rewarding, as the type of children's theater presentation that is discussed in the next chapter.

Both readers theater and conventional plays provide excellent opportunities for practice in silent and oral reading skills, the study of language and literature, training for body expression, practice in characterization and script analysis, development of self confidence and poise, and fostering a sense of teamwork toward shared goals. But because they use only minimal costuming and scenery, readers theater productions are far less expensive and complicated to coordinate, schedule and stage.

A readers theater production can be rehearsed and performed in an ordinary classroom. This eliminates the often frustrating problem of finding and scheduling rehearsal space. In addition, it is easy for students aged ten and older to have a major hand in creating their own scripts from readily available sources.

What Is Readers Theater?

Readers theater is a minimally staged interpretation of a script developed from many kinds of literature such as poems, plays, stories, etc. The script can be adapted or cut from a single work or it can be

Students discuss a fine point during a readers theater rehearsal.

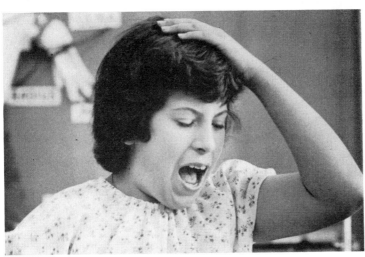

Despite the term *readers* theater, students memorize their lines and do not hold their scripts in their hands during performance. In this picture, a piece of sky has just fallen on Chicken Little.

compiled from various sources and organized to illustrate a theme, tell a story or explore a mood.

The form is used in many colleges and universities as a teaching device in theater, speech, history, English and foreign language classes. In more and more elementary and junior high school classes, readers theater is providing the same kind of springboard for learning that conventional children's theater has traditionally offered.

Despite the term *readers* theater, students memorize their lines and do not hold their scripts in their hands during performance. Part of the convention is that each student can perform more than one role in any play. Staging is simple yet imaginative, with no attempt at realism. Whenever possible, expressive movement provides the necessary transitions and explanations. Rarely, if ever, does readers theater call for costumes, scenery or specialized lighting. Theatrical effects depend largely on the quality of the oral reading and on the clarity, precision and expressiveness of the stage movement.

How to Create Scripts

Very few companies publish readers theater scripts suitable for performance by and for young people. (Some are available from Arthur Meriwether, Inc., Box 457, Downers Grove, Illinois 60515). However, it is easy for students to create their own scripts under the editorial guidance of their teacher. Any literature appropriate for your students' age level will make fine readers theater material.

The works of Dr. Seuss, for example, are particularly good for most elementary students. The stories contain clear characterization and a taut story line that will help hold the audience's attention. Most of his works can easily be cut to suit your own needs in terms of playing time, the number of lines to be learned by each student and the attention span of the audience. I have seen several highly entertaining readers theater versions of *Horton Hatches the Egg*.

The *Horton* script is taken from a single source. Any anthology of children's poems or plays will provide usable material for scripts drawn from various sources. A particularly good one is Geraldine Brain Siks' *Children's Literature for Dramatization: An Anthology* (Harper and Row, 1964). "The World of Animals," "The Colors around Us," and "City Life" are some possible titles of scripts made up of selections with unifying themes. For this type of script, you may need to include some narration coupled with expressive movement that provide explanations and/or transitions to keep the performance fluid and intelligible.

For both types of scripts remember that, unlike most children's theater scripts, literature for readers theater need not contain such inherently dramatic qualities as dialogue and physical action. On the other hand, opportunities for creating dramatic interplay between characters and expressive movement should exist. You and the students can then prepare the script so that these qualities will emerge.

For example, one student may be directed to speak one line of the script, the whole cast the next line, three people the third and so forth. Whenever possible, the director should add movement or action that helps develop the characters' motivations and the meaning of the spoken words. A knowledge of the kinds of blocking techniques discussed in Chapter Four is vital.

To illustrate how to transform a poem into suitable readers theater material, I have chosen a verse of "My Shadow" by Robert Louis Stevenson:

Six students enter the classroom singing "Side by Side." ("We ain't got a barrel of money. Maybe we're ragged and funny," etc.) Three students wearing white trousers and white turtlenecks are the "people". Three wearing dark trousers and turtlenecks are the "shadows." (Such costuming is, of course, optional.) They enter in black and white pairs. When they reach the front of the room, they stand in two rows facing away from the audience, with the "people" row closer to the audience. As the song ends, the "people" turn around.

PERSON 1: I have a little shadow that goes . . . (all "people" gesture to the left, to "shadow" 1)

SHADOW 1: (takes a step to left, turns to face audience) In . . .

ALL "PEOPLE": (in unison) And . . . (gesture to the right)

SHADOW 2: (takes a step to the right, facing the audience) Out . . .

ALL "PEOPLE": (in unison) With me.

SHADOW 3: (turns, crosses through the "people" and addresses the audience) And what can be the use of him (gestures to the "people") is more than I can see.

PERSON 2: (moves to left of "shadow" 3, who is center stage) He is very, very like me . . .

PERSON 3: (moves to right of "shadow" 3) From the heels up to the head.

PERSON 1: (moves to a chair on stage left) And I can see him jump before me . . .

SHADOW 3: (moves from stage center to a chair on stage right) When I jump into my bed.

The completed script should be typed in standard script form so that it clearly indicates who speaks what lines. Provide each cast member with a script. All the participants will need to be aware of what everyone else is saying and have a complete knowledge of their own lines.

The finished script should read as a definable unit with a clear beginning and a definite ending. The latter is particularly important if the script is a collage of works or an adaptation of one particular work. The ending should provide both a logical and a theatrical conclusion. The audience should never have to guess when the performance is over. A simple solution is to have the performers bow and/or exit.

How Long?

For students aged eleven and younger, between ten and thirty minutes of playing time is most effective. If you double-space a script on standard 8½" x 11" pages, you can plan on approximately two and one-half minutes of performance time per printed page.

The length of the script will depend on how much material you and the students want to include. Be sure to exclude material that doesn't suit the overall purpose or theme of the script. Guide the students towards more materials if they do not have enough suggestions.

What Size Cast?

If you will be performing in a small area, you must be sure to leave ample space for expressive movement. In such cases, the number of readers should not exceed ten or twelve.

Although you may tend to select the best oral readers for the biggest roles, keep in mind that readers theater often acts as a strong motivation for students with reading problems. Try to include such students whenever possible by assigning them smaller parts that challenge their abilities.

Directing Hints

The readers theater director strives to suggest illusions to the audience rather than to present an elaborate, visual spectacle. Staging relies on the imaginative use of voice, movement, and a few simple props rather than on costumes or scenery. A group of chairs placed in a straight line can suggest a bus, a subway car or a classroom. A single chair can become a table, a platform, a mountain, a tall building, the branch of a tree or an airplane cockpit. The audience will believe it to be whatever the actors believe it to be.

In readers theater, dramatic effects depend largely on the quality of the oral reading and on the clarity, precision and expression of the stage movement.

The same principle holds true for action, or blocking. Actions and movements in readers theater are suggestive and muted rather than realistic and highly detailed as in conventional theater. As a result, eye contact between characters and expressive use of arms, hands, legs, and bodies take on an expanded significance.

Background noise and action also help spectators visualize the imaginary world that is being created for them. In a scene set in a factory, the performers can move their arms and legs with mechanical precision (up and down, in circles, etc.) to suggest a large and complicated piece of machinery. A city scene can be given extra vividness when the students imitate the sounds of horns, automobiles and trains. The same thing can be done with the rural sounds of birds, animals, the wind, and so on.

Narration must provide smooth transitions between sections of the written script; imaginative blocking must provide effective and believable transitions from one part of the performance to the next. For instance, if actors drop character, then turn and face away from the audience, the spectators will understand that they have "exited" from a scene. When they reassume their characters and face the audience again, it will be understood that they have reentered.

Once you can work with this kind of "suggested" as opposed to "realistic" staging, the solution to many so-called technical problems will be well within your grasp. With a few stools or chairs and lots of imagination, you and your students can create any action, at any place, at any time.

The best source for many other specific ideas on staging readers theater is *Readers Theatre Handbook: A Dramatic Approach to Literature* (rev. ed.) by Leslie Irene Coger and Melvin R. White (Scott, Foresman, 1973). Designed as a college text, it is an invaluable source of both basic and advanced techniques.

Conclusion

Readers theater, like puppet theater, is a distinct art. Like all forms of theater, it relies ultimately on its actors and is an excellent medium for training young performers. Freed from worries about sets, costumes, make-up, and so forth, they can concentrate on the elements of script analysis, characterization, voice and movement that are the fundamentals of the actor's art.

10

Basic Production Techniques

People who teach acting in schools and recreation departments are often expected to direct some kind of final production. The principal, the parents and the students themselves usually expect and frequently demand that a program of acting lessons culminate in the production of a play. Teachers need to understand that directing a play involves a lot more than just working with actors.

A character on a popular children's television series once described a director as someone who "kinda makes a lot of noise and tells everyone what to do." Theater director/teachers—whether dealing with children or not—are often thought of as authority figures who set up rehearsal schedules and exhort the actors to learn their lines, feel their parts and believe in what they are doing. The good director is usually perceived as someone who is sensitive and articulate, someone who can provide a *creative* atmosphere in which the actors, designers and technicians can work, someone who understands and addresses the human spirit.

At first glance, this point of view seems perfectly reasonable. Such a definition, however, is both flawed and incomplete.

Before they can possibly be *creative*, director/teachers must possess a wide range of theatrical experience, knowledge and technique that is firmly grounded in a love and respect for the arts of theater. Just as important, good teacher/directors are first administrators—organizers— and then artists. A director's capacity and willingness to organize and

115

preplan rehearsals can save time and conserve a great deal of emotional and physical energy.

Once the decision to "do a play" has been made, there are many questions to be answered. What kind of play—puppet, readers theater, participation drama, or straight childrens theater? Should it be a musical, a comedy, a tragedy or a melodrama? The final decision depends on a variety of things. Among them are the tastes and preferences of the teacher and students, the sex, number and ages of the available performers, the scene and costume requirements, the quality of the rehearsal and performance facilities, the budget, and the nature of the proposed audience.

The teacher/director will want to note how long the play is. How many male and how many female roles does it have? Will it appeal to the students who will have to rehearse and perform it? Is it within their artistic range? How often, when and where will rehearsals take place?

Is it a royalty play? In other words, must a fee be paid before the play can legally be performed? If it is a royalty free-play, it will normally be so labelled. If a royalty payment is required, the fact that yours may be a classroom, nonprofit or educational performance does not necessarily exempt you from the financial, legal and moral responsibilities of paying for its use. Inexperienced directors are often unpleasantly surprised and extremely embarrassed when they or their principals or supervisors receive a bill for performance rights after the performance is over. Large play publishers usually employ clipping services—and even the smallest article about your performance in the most out-of-the-way newspaper has a good chance of winding up in the billing department of the play's publisher. Publishing plays is their business and they're serious about it.

There is a way to avoid this problem. Free catalogues of both royalty and royalty-free plays are available upon request from a number of reputable publishers. These include but are not limited to:

Baker's Play Publishing Co.
100 Chauncy St.
Boston, Mass. 02110

Contemporary Drama Service
Box 457
Downers Grove, Illinois 60515

Dramatic Publishing Co.
86 E. Randolph
Chicago, Illinois 60601

Dramatists Play Services Inc.
440 Park Ave. South
New York, New York 10016

Eldridge Publishing Co.
P.O. Drawer 209
Franklyn, Ohio 45005

Samuel French
25 W. 45th St.
New York, New York 10036

Heuer Publishing Co.
233 Dows Building
P.O. Box 248
Cedar Rapids, Iowa 52406

David McKay Co.
Play Dept.
750 3rd Ave.
New York, New York 10017

Performance Publishing
978 McLean Blvd.
Elgin, Illinois 60120

Pickwick Plays
3524 Rockdale Ct.
Baltimore, Maryland 21207

New Plays for Children
P.O. Box 273
Rowayton, Conn. 06853

Anchorage Press, Inc.
Anchorage, Kentucky 40223

The catalogues of these publishers are regularly updated or supplemented. Current issues of them are basic tools of the trade and they belong in the library of anyone interested in doing theater for the young performer. They provide valuable information about the plays such as scene and costume requirements, reading level, number and sex of characters, playing time, and royalty fees. A quick reading of the catalogue description will also help the director plan for any necessary assistants such as musicians, choreographers, scene and/or costume designers, lighting technicians, gymnastic advisors, or extra assistants for supervising large casts.

There is a wide variety of plays ranging from those which are technically simple, royalty free and have small casts to those which are expensive, have large casts and are technically complicated. It is wise to pick a play that you are *positive* you can produce. In other words, if you don't have a skilled and reliable costumer, musical director or have no way to deal with special lighting or scenery, pick a play that doesn't depend on these elements. Such plays exist. Search through the catalogues to find them or write your own scripts.

Although plays vary widely in terms of settings, costumes and lighting, all plays—no matter what type—must be analyzed and blocked. One of the most persistent and least understood problems of many theater teacher/directors is blocking—the movement of the performers around the stage with relationship to one another and to the stage setting.

It is one thing for a director to exort a student to read "more expressively" and quite another—and better—thing for the director to guide the student, through intelligent use of movement towards the desired improvement. Some examples of expressive movement patterns and other blocking suggestions were discussed in Chapter Four.

So important is blocking that many directors routinely complete detailed blocking plans long before the play is even cast. The degree to which the movement is preplanned is certain to save hours of valuable rehearsal time.

While the difficulty of preplanning the blocking will vary from play to play, the mechanics are really quite simple. At the outset, the director should prepare or have prepared a one-quarter-inch scale drawing of the plan of the set (or sets). A plan is a scale drawing of the set as viewed from above. Without such a plan it is virtually impossible to preplan the blocking. From this point, there are many methods.

I mount the set plan on a piece of cardboard so that it will lie flat on a table. Then I gather some dimes. On each dime I paste a small label with the name of the character written on it—one dime for each character in the play. I read through the script with these materials in front of me and move the dimes as I would wish the actors on stage to move, noting each movement in a special "shorthand" in a prompt script.

In order to make a prompt script, you will need two copies of the script. Cut the pages out of the script and tape the pages onto larger sheets of paper placed on the right hand side of a loose leaf binder. You will need two scripts because most books are printed on both sides of the page. It is convenient for the left-hand leaf to be left blank in order to provide space

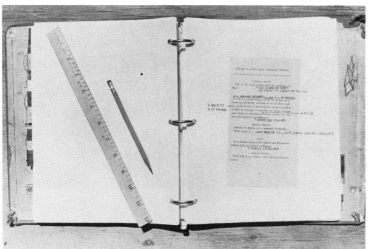

A neatly prepared prompt script is an important production tool. It contains all the major blocking instructions and technical cues.

for any additional notes and diagrams that apply to the page of script and blocking notes.

All movement away from the audience—whether in a direct line or an angle—is called *upstage* movement, for which the common symbol is U. All movement toward the audience—whether in a straight line or an angle is called *downstage* movement, for which the common symbol is D. The symbol ↓ is used when people sit, a ↑ is used when they stand. A movement from one place to another on stage is called a cross—an X is the obvious symbol. Right (R) and left (L) refer to the *performers'* right and left as though they were facing the audience. Center (C) refers to the center of the stage. The name of each character in the blocking instructions is usually shortened to its first two letters.

Thus, the direction "Dorothy gets up from the couch and walks down stage left to the up right of the Cowardly Lion" can easily and nearly be written into the margin of the script as: Do ↑ couch XDL to UR of CoLi." Each direction is written *in pencil*—directions change during rehearsal. They are written in the margin of the script, with a line drawn with a ruler to the exact place in the script where the movement should occur:

Do ↑ couch XDL to UR of COLI   Dorothy: Oh| you poor thing!

If there are stage directions already indicated in the script, they may, but *need not* be used. They may, in fact, have been written for a stage or setting much different from the one you are using.

In any case, the blocking should always be recorded either by the director or a stage manager in the prompt script. Failure to record the blocking directions usually means that no one will remember from one rehearsal to the next where the performers are supposed to go or what they are supposed to do at any particular moment. With older students, grades four and up, it is a good idea to teach all performers how to record their blocking in their own scripts.

Picking the right play, analyzing the script, and planning the blocking are only some of the important steps in organizing the processes of rehearsal and production.

Rehearsals themselves are easy to schedule. As much as possible, try to avoid asking students to come to rehearsals when their presence is not absolutely required. At the first rehearsal, the cast may simply read the play aloud with each actor performing his or her assigned role. This is also the time for the director to introduce the actors to any technical staff and to outline everyone's job responsibilities, deadlines and their functions within the total production scheme.

The next phase of rehearsals is devoted to giving the actors their blocking. In these sessions, the students move through, write down and learn the basic movements of the show—who goes where and exactly when. Work on blocking will continue until the last stage of rehearsal. The blocking will improve and become more detailed as everyone becomes increasingly familiar with the characters, the lines, the major actions and the general flow of the production. If the director has carefully pre-planned and clearly recorded most of the movement, the initial blocking rehearsals for a forty-five minute performance should take between three and six hours.

Well before blocking rehearsals are completed, the director should give all the actors a clear idea of when they are to have lines and blocking for every scene committed to memory. Tell the actors and then write down the schedule and post it in some agreed upon place. For example:

"Mon., March 12 3:00-4:30 p.m.: Run through, Scene 1 OFF BOOK
    Scene 1 characters: Mayor, Good Witch, Billy, Gray Knight, Mrs.
        Ogleby

Tues., March 13 3:00-4:30 p.m.: Run through, Scene 2 OFF BOOK
    Scene 2 characters: Mayor, Widgin family, Billy, Gray Knight,
        Good Witch, Maria.

During subsequent rehearsals, cast members, guided by the director, will try to understand their characters' thoughts and motivations. This will help them to perform their roles with greater expertise and

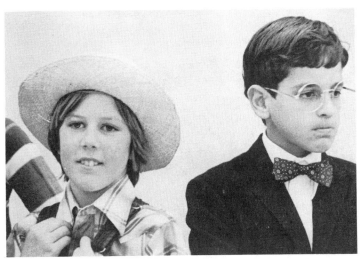

People who teach acting in schools and recreation departments are often expected to direct some kind of final production. Scene from *Tom Sawyer*.

conviction. At this time, the students will also learn how to coordinate their lines and emotions with their blocking. They will also try to develop greater sensitivity to what the other characters are saying and doing.

The first day of the last week of rehearsals is usually the first *technical* rehearsal. At this time, the actors are introduced to the costumes, lights and sets as they will appear in the final performance. It usually takes a few days before everyone can work comfortably with all of the technical elements. Undoubtedly, problems will arise which may necessitate rethinking or reblocking portions of some scenes. The last two or three rehearsals before *dress rehearsal* is the time to make these final changes. *Dress rehearsal* is simply a performance without an audience, and by this time everyone—actors as well as backstage crew—should know what they are doing. A dress rehearsal provides an important psychological bridge between the processes of rehearsal and those of performance. Major changes introduced at this point will usually not be of much use—particularly if only one or two performances have been scheduled. Such last minute alterations will tend to confuse and fluster everyone and will make the opening performance more—rather than less—difficult. It is sometimes a good idea to arrange for a small group of spectators to be present at the dress rehearsal in order to help the actors get used to playing in front of an audience. They will need to get used to reacting to an audience's applause or laughter.

If the performance is to be held in a room that is *not* the normal classroom/rehearsal area, then the exact times and dates for this use of the space should be worked out well in advance. In some larger

A completely staged production requires a great deal of work from a great many people. Scene from *Tom Sawyer*.

elementary, junior high or high schools, the multi-purpose rooms are used as a combination gymnasium/cafeteria/auditorium. Such rooms are so busy that it is sometimes necessary to reserve them as much as a year in advance. In addition, you will want to know ahead of time whether or not you will have to remove the set from the room between rehearsals and performances.

If you are going to use some kind of special lighting, you will want to find out well beforehand exactly what you and the lighting system can and cannot do. Who will run the lights during performance? Can the room be completely darkened during the day? Can you find a trustworthy person to whom you can delegate the responsibility of handling any difficult or peculiar lighting problems?

Much the same is true of costumes and scenery. Who will do the designing? Who will do the building? Where will the completed materials be stored? How will scene and costume changes be accomplished without disturbing the flow of the production? Can regular meetings be scheduled between the director and the designers so that everyone will know what the entire production staff is doing in order to discover and correct errors on time?

Whenever possible, it is always best to centralize the responsibility for the technical aspects of the performance. Some *one* competent person should be in charge of lights, some one competent person should be in charge of the lights and set. The director's responsibility is to organize and schedule these people so that they can work together as a team and complete their various duties on time. It is usually impossible for directors to perform all technical jobs themselves.

The director should also be a diplomat who can settle conflicts, soothe wounded feelings and avoid difficult situations before they arise. A great portion of the director's time is taken up with apparently mundane but extremely important tasks such as making lists, working up and writing schedules, and constantly yet forcefully seeing to it that everyone associated with the play is working adequately and according to plan. Even that most persistent problem of motivating the students to learn their lines is usually minimized when they are working with or around adults who are prepared, knowledgeable, organized, and obviously working hard on the tasks at hand.

Although it is a fact that beginners often overlook, a completely staged production requires a great deal of work from a great many people. It is the director's job to keep them working effectively and working together. In addition, a full production provides the best possible laboratory experience for student actors. It is, of course, the ultimate purpose of the actor's art.

Conclusion

All artists address the human spirit. What distinguishes them from other people is the degree to which they have mastered their own particular ways of organizing their skills and communicating with their audiences. Colorful splotches on a piece of paper are not necessarily paintings and someone who knows nothing and cares less about color, form, composition and brushstrokes can scarcely lay claim to being very much of a painter. An individual who cannot carry a tune, read or write music, or play any particular instrument would obviously have a good deal of difficulty persuading audiences that he or she was a musician. Random and marginally organized sound does not necessarily qualify as music. By the same token, an event in which people more or less memorize some lines, don costumes, and move through a particular stage space does not necessarily constitute a work of theater art. Yet teachers who have little or no knowledge and experience with or about theater often persuade themselves as well as their employers that their "creative urges" and good intentions adequately equip them to teach acting or other theater arts to children.

Enthusiasm and desire, although they are important prerequisites, are adjuncts to, not substitutes for, theatrical knowledge, experience and technique. Like the teachers of other arts, the acting teacher/director should understand and be at least moderately knowledgeable about the art before undertaking the responsibility of teaching it. There is no point in adding to society's quotient of well-meaning theatrical enthusiasts who so frequently mistake ignorance for originality and a random flow of half-defined or poorly expressed ideas for creativity and artistic expression.

This does not mean that everyone who teaches theater for young people has to devote their lives and souls to teaching theater and nothing else. No one expects the teacher who introduces students to the fundamentals of reading and writing to be a brilliant poet or novelist. Of course, no one wants reading teachers who are complete illiterates, either.

This book was written for directors and acting teachers. As its title promised, it has offered a number of practical ideas and exercises which have been designed to introduce students between the ages of seven and fourteen to the art of acting. Some of the requisite skills and ideas are relatively easy to explain or acquire, others are more difficult. It is hoped that teachers who are interested in teaching acting to young people will be able to guide and temper their teaching of fundamental skills with an understanding of some of the more complicated issues. For example, although it might be difficult to teach the chapter on blocking to students younger than eleven or twelve, a teacher could make use of the knowledge and techniques in that chapter to help develop the skills of eight or nine year olds.

The point of the exercises in this book is to train actors. In the intensity of their desire to become better actors, a number of poor readers or speakers will become motivated to improve their reading or speaking skills, shy students may learn to enjoy performing in public and, as a result, overcome some of their shyness, and so forth. If such students can use their interest in acting to help solve such problems, so much the better.

Acting texts that promise to give readers "everything they need to know" are misleading. At best, a book can only provide some possibilities for organizing and using knowledge that the acting teacher/director should accumulate in a variety of additional places and ways. It is my hope that the possibilities outlined in this book will prove useful to those who want to direct and teach acting to young people.

Index